John Newey

Pc 6

Rotherham Borough Police & Beyond......

Copyright © 2018

By

John Newey

True stories of young constable in 1965 in Rotherham Borough Police and in Sheffield and Rotherham Constabulary.

Recalling 4 decades in South Yorkshire Police, involving murders, firearms, robbery and assaults.

The recollections in this book are all true accounts. However, some of the names of those involved have been changed to protect their privacy.

Chapters

Some of the proceeds from the sale of my book will be donated to Shiloh Rotherham, an organisation which helps the disadvantaged, and where I volunteer. A donation will also be made to NARPO Rotherham (National Association of Retired Police Officers).

INTRODUCTION & ACKNOWLEDGMENTS

This is a collection of my memories.
I've enjoyed every one.

I wish to thank my beloved parents and my grandmother **Beatrice**.

I've met so many people in my lifetime and the following in particular have given me great love, help, support.

My ex wife **Lee**, **Toni** and **Ray Mountford**. **Sam** and **Martin Scott**. **Peter** and **Lynn Moxon**. **Eric Twigg**. **Stuart Rushton** and **Doreen Lidster**.
These people are gone, but will never be forgotten.
Tony Scruby. **John Hughes**. **Derek Dalton** and **Roy Jenkins**.

My special thanks for their amazing help and assistance in the preparation and production of my book goes to **Jeannette Hensby**, author and crime writer. **Martyn Sharpe**, author and retired Sun newspaper crime writer and **Robin Alexander Eadon**, author and writer of the 'Captain Thomas' series of children's books.

John Newey

Chapter 1
In The Beginning

A year after the end of World War Two, in the early Spring of 1946, I was born in Swinton in the West Riding of Yorkshire, later to become South Yorkshire. The town was in the heart of the Yorkshire coalfield and whilst not having a colliery of its own, Manvers Main, Kilnhurst, Silverwood, Denaby and Wath were all situated nearby.

My father, Bill, was from neighbouring Mexborough and my mother, Beatrice, was from Swinton. They had both played their respective roles in the war. He was a Stoker 1st class in the Royal Navy, serving on the convoys to Murmansk and Archangel. My mother worked locally at Baker and Bessemer at Kilnhurst helping to make munitions for the war effort.

After the war ended, my dad resumed working at Barnburgh and Manvers collieries as a coal face ripper. He and his brave colleagues operated at the sharp end with picks and shovels, as mechanisation was very limited in the late 1940's and 1950's.

As an infant we moved to Bowbroom, an area of Swinton, to live in a prefabricated bungalow. I remember my dad had a pedal cycle and he fashioned a seat for me; attaching it to the crossbar so I could accompany him on a Friday to the wages office at Manvers Main colliery where he worked as a coal face ripper. I was entrusted with his pit check brass ID disc, which had to be produced to obtain his pay. We would often cycle over the open land known as the plantation to reach the colliery. This common land was the home, for two weeks in the summer, to a dozen or so pit ponies who enjoyed a well-earned break from their underground hell hole, dragging coal carts on the mines rail network. Many of the local kids, me included, took bread, carrots and apples to feed them, along with buckets of water. A couple of them let us ride them.

We moved to Brookfield Avenue in Swinton on my 6th birthday to occupy a semi-detached council house right next door to my maternal grandmother. She was a beacon in my life. The centre of the garden had an air raid shelter which my dad filled in with rubble. I often wondered if it had been used in the war years.

My dad's parents lived in Mexborough and on Christmas eve 1953 we visited them to deliver presents. I was excited maybe still believing in Father Christmas! At 8pm we walked back to catch a bus home. I was holding my dad's hand and felt his grip tighten and he stopped walking. He was holding his head, then collapsed to the ground. I remember my mother sending me to get help to my grandparents. Somehow we got home. I thought all was well, but by mid-morning on Christmas day an ambulance arrived to take my dad to the Northern

General Hospital in Sheffield. I later learned he had an inoperable brain tumour, and It was just a matter of time. My mother visited him every day for three years until he didn't know anyone. He died at Rotherham, 1st February 1959, aged 35. I missed him so very much, especially playing football for the school. All my pals' dads were there, except mine. There wasn't any counselling back then; you just got on with it.

My mother had three jobs to make ends meet. One on the "twilight shift" 7 – 9.30pm at the GEC white goods factory in Swinton, where she was on the toasters and kettles production line. She also had two part time jobs at local grocery shops in the town.

My Nan Thompson was such an important part of my formative years and I owe such a lot to my mother and nan. It was never easy for them. Money was tight but I wanted for nothing.

My dad's pit service qualified us for widows' coal following his passing. The home coal delivery lorry was a very welcome sight every quarter, especially in the harsh winter months. The tipper lorry would drop a ton of mixed-doubles coal off outside the house. Mixed-doubles was a grade of coal suitable for domestic use. A near neighbour, Mr Cooke, a white haired elderly gentleman could always be called upon for a small fee and a token free barrow of coal to get the coal in for any neighbours. At 12 years of age I decided to get the coal in myself, which meant shovelling it into a barrow, pushing it a few yards to the back of the house and shovelling it into the coal place. So one ton became a two ton task, but it was good exercise and fitness building

My education comprised of a year at Haugh Road Rawmarsh, before a move to a newly built school at Swinton where new friends were made. I did okay at most subjects at school, but football was my favourite sport and it was my ambition to become a professional. A number of my peers were very good players and local scouts were keen to invite us to professional clubs for trials. Peter Taylor was a local man who worked as a scout for several professional clubs and he took me to Barnsley, Derby County and Wolverhampton Wanderers for trials, but all came to nothing. I played for Swinton Youth Club and we swept all before us, winning leagues and cups with relative ease. A team mate, Harry Good, was a promising goalkeeper and Taylor told us a scout from the famous Premiership club Everton FC wanted us to go to Liverpool for further assessment. It was an amazing opportunity at such a glamorous club.

Upon arrival at Goodison Park Stadium, we were met by staff who took us to meet the manager, Mr Harry Catterick, who also managed Sheffield Wednesday. His office had oak panelled walls displaying team pictures, and there was a trophy cabinet with silverware and pennants from European clubs they had played. I was truly awestruck. Mr Catterick was sitting behind his huge desk, which was covered with paperwork and various football programmes. He welcomed Harry and myself to the famous old club and outlined the itinerary for the day ahead.

We joined the rest of the junior players and changed in the away dressing room, with the senior professionals using the home dressing room, and then we all boarded the Everton FC team coach for the short journey to Bellfield training ground. We passed slowly by some roadworks and the road crew, recognising the coach, quickly brought out their red and white flags and scarves to taunt us in a good natured way; to show us their allegiance to Liverpool FC.

Upon arrival at Bellfield, the Coach, Tommy Egglestone, picked the teams for the game ahead. I wore an Everton club shirt carrying number six on the back and lined up with England and Scotland international players: Gordon West, Brian Labone, Colin Harvey and Alex Young. If I wasn't overawed before, I certainly was now!

The opposition had Tony Kay in their line-up who quickly left his mark upon my leg. The game was over very quickly, and I realised the huge gulf between my limited abilities and their obvious levels of class. But it was an experience of a lifetime to even be there on the same pitch as these soccer greats.

On the journey back, the flame haired Tony Kay, ex England and Sheffield Wednesday, had acquired a large bucket of iced water and was standing next to the coach driver, telling him to stop when we reached the road workers who quickly took out their scarves to taunt the Everton bus. As if it was slow motion, Kay slid open the bus door and drenched one of the Liverpool fans in the ice cold water. It was an hilarious moment; even they took it in good part. I wonder what the Football Association's reaction would be if such a prank was carried out in today's world.

Mr Catterick was waiting for us back at the stadium. He was a gentleman and generous with his time, thanking us for coming, explaining that we needed to keep practising. A really nice way of putting us on the road home.

I was still playing at Swinton Youth Club and along with a team mate, Richard England, we were selected for an FA (Football Association) course in Surrey, where our coach was George Curtis, the then manager of Stevenage FC. George identified some ability in both of us and invited us to visit the Hertfordshire club and Richard and I subsequently signed as professional players for the club on £5 per week wages. The club found me some digs with Tom and Mary Ince, who were Northern people and made me very welcome, although I did suffer some homesickness. My injury woes would soon resurface, and the club paid for my physiotherapy under the care of Geoff Goodhall at Sheffield United. He thought I had returned to playing too soon with shin splints and hamstring plaguing me again. Perhaps my injuries were due to growth spurts in my early years when muscles outgrow bone. Shin spurts affected me as well. If I'd received more information by medical experts, things may have been different. As it was, I often played instead of resting to aid recovery. I learned Curtis was lining me up for a money move to Millwall FC, but they wouldn't invest in an injured player. Knowing this, the club paid for me to visit a Harley Street specialist to try and resolve my problems. The prognosis was not good. I had been out injured for months and I knew the club wouldn't continue paying me for too much longer. Eventually my contract was cancelled by mutual consent and I was paid up. My dream of a career in football lay in ruins. I had a season playing semi-professional for Denaby United in the Midland League before I decided to call it a day.

I always harboured an ambition to repay my mother for the many sacrifices she made bringing me up. In 1984, with the blessing and support of my former wife Lee, we bought the Council house I was raised in, enabling my mother to live rent free for the rest of her life. It was of little consolation, but at least Lee and I were with her when she passed peacefully away at 4pm on Wednesday 25th September 2002.

That day was a watershed in my life.

Chapter 2
Career Choice Time

My first job was as an office boy at the National Coal Board Finance Dept. at Denaby near Doncaster. I had left school at Easter and was only just turned 15 years old I got my first wage packet of £3.15s.6d. which I handed to my mother for board and lodging expenses.

Apart from a couple of school play ground romances, I hadn't had a steady girlfriend until I was just turned nineteen when I met Janette Moore, who was a shorthand typist in the Stores Department at the same offices. We dated for a few years and got engaged; broke it off; got engaged a second time and broke it off again. Maybe it was too early for both of us to consider marriage and we went our separate ways.

I was getting a bit stir crazy being confined to the office and the work was repetitive and tedious. I needed a new challenge. I perhaps didn't give my job change enough serious thought before attending an interview at a Sheffield steelworks. It was for a clerical position paying about two pounds per week more than the NCB, but after bus fares had been taken into account, it was virtually the same wages as I was getting. I walked back into Rotherham and whilst waiting for my bus back to Swinton, I saw two policemen talking outside the Rotherham Borough Police HQ's on Frederick Street. I had never considered becoming a policeman, but thought I'd call at the front desk and enquire if they had any vacancies. I was eventually met by Inspector Bramhall, the officer in charge of recruitment. He asked me if I was available to sit the police entrance examination lasting about two hours. I was, and found the English, maths and general knowledge papers relatively straightforward. The Inspector marked each subject, and told me I'd achieved the required mark.

In September 1965 I received a letter from the Chief Constable S.W. Morris offering me a position in the force subject to a medical, which was a formality. A new career beckoned which really came out of the blue so to speak.

On 11th October 1965 I was sworn into the office of constable before Frank Beardshall JP, in the Rotherham Magistrates' Court at Frederick Street, Rotherham. I picked up The Holy Bible, and with Neil Anthony Cooke, the Clerk to the Court saying the oath, I repeated after him:

"I John William Newey do solemnly and sincerely declare and affirm that I will well and truly serve The Queen in the office of Constable with fairness, integrity, diligence and impartiality

upholding fundamental human rights and according equal respect to all people; and that I will to the best of my power cause the peace to be kept and preserved and prevent all offences against people and property; and that while I continue to hold the said office I will to the best of my skill and knowledge, discharge all the duties thereof faithfully according to law."

Inspector Bramhall decided upon my collar numbers to be worn on my uniform and he as Pc/Sgt had number 6 and wanted me to wear it. I felt honoured. I had to have a friend come to help me carry home my uniform issue: Summer/winter weight tunics and trousers, Sanforized blue shirts with detachable collars, Greatcoats, helmets, gloves, torch, truncheon, handcuffs and boots. The weight of just the minimum clothing was too heavy to carry.

Prior to attending my initial training I was allowed out in full uniform under the strict supervision of an experienced constable. We walked for miles and I soon got heel blisters, my legs ached with the heavy serge full uniform, but I was determined I'd overcome any obstacles in my way. A mile or so out of town was a police section office at Ferham. It was a small office with a table and chairs in the public area, and a private mess room with a simple kitchen and toilet. Three beat officers on a 24hrs shift cycle would operate from there. I reported for duty at 1.45pm for a 2 –10pm shift and, in company with Pc Bill Brown, we commenced foot patrol onto the Kimberworth beat.

A regular thing on most officers agenda was to stop and check motor vehicles - lorries cars and motor cycles - to ensure the driver was lawfully in possession of the vehicle and that documents were in order. Occasionally motorists carried ID; driving licence, insurance and test certificate, but in cases where they hadn't, a small duplicated form called HO/RT/1 would be issued for their production within 7 days at a police station of their choice.

I stopped my very first vehicle, a blue Commer van being driven on Kimberworth Road by a lady called Susan Craven. I had employed the number one police stop signal with the van a few yards away by stepping into the road and, in the prescribed manner, held my right arm vertically to complete the stop. My heart was pounding, my throat dry, and I tried to bring to memory the standard opening gambit:

"Good afternoon, this is a routine check, can I see your driving documents please?"

The van stopped and the female driver slid the door open. I'd managed to start my sentence when I was hit by a torrent of verbal abuse like a hair dryer on full power. Mrs Craven said,

"What the fuck do you want, ain't yer got owt better to fucking do? Go and catch some fucking robbers."

I truly hadn't heard a woman speak and act so aggressively before and was quite taken aback. I was at a loss for words, muttering something to her about her documents. It crossed my mind that maybe I'd chosen the wrong career if everyone was going to react like her! Pc Brown came to my aid and asked her why she was acting so aggressively. She gave him a similar volley of expletives before she calmed down and accepted a HO/RT/1 electing to produce at Rotherham. She produced all the documents, in order, the following day.

My colleague assured me that not everyone would be so abusive and she perhaps detected I was a brand new recruit. I met her on subsequent occasions, each time at Bradgate Motors, a quarry-based car wreckers yard that Susan co-owned with her husband, Alan. She was generally better mannered but had a short fuse.

Several years later I was doing a prison visit at HMP Lindholme near Doncaster, when I saw Alan who was working in the prison canteen as a trustee inmate. I knew he was unable to read or write, but his cell mate, Ken Priestfield, acted as his scribe; writing letters home to Susan for him. It transpired Susan and Priestfield were conducting an illicit affair initially by post, but upon his release their association developed into a full blown relationship. The two-timing Priestfield was also carrying on with a younger lover and killed Susan (54) so he could get her £1 million pound will. He showed his girlfriend Susan's body saying, "I did it to be with you". He threatened her that, should she say anything, he'd kill her and her family. Priestfield was charged with murdering Susan without her body being found, but two days later police found her head inside a concrete block. He had butchered her body which was never found. The jury who convicted Priestfield were later told Susan's killer had already served time for trying to murder his wife and daughter for a £55,000 insurance payout. He had hired two hit-men and in 1984 got ten years imprisonment. A seriously dangerous man whose crime the judge described, "as a calculated cold blooded attempt at murder". Yet he was released to eventually kill Susan Craven.

Chapter 3
Police Training School

On Monday 18th October 1965 all my bags were packed ready to go. My mother and girlfriend, Janette drove me to the number 3 Police District Training Centre at Pannal Ash, Harrogate, North Yorkshire. This was my home for my 13 weeks initial training. I truly had no idea what I should expect beyond the classroom and parade ground. Pannal Ash was like a miniature stately home with imposing buildings and manicured gardens, sports fields and a separate swimming pool. The self-contained main block consisted of classrooms, main hall and dining hall on the ground floor, and bedrooms and dormitories on the second floor. I was fortunate to have my own room which overlooked the rolling countryside in the distance and the parade square immediately below. The first day was registration and general administration, followed by Sergeant Foster, the drill sergeant, giving a demonstration of bed pack making. I must admit I wasn't too familiar with much household chores, thanks to my mother's expertise in that field. Making a bed pack was a daily task involving the exact folding of bedsheets, with the wrap around counterpane completing the process. In the early days we performed like contestants on Bruce Forsyth's 'Generation Game' who had to complete a task with limited ability. Our shortcomings in achieving the required precision finish were brutally exposed when Sgt Foster's pay-stick poked into the stack of bedding and threw them onto the floor. It was part of the introduction to discipline that was the underlying theme to life at the centre. Sgt Foster, I am sure, had undergone surgery to remove his ability to smile. His police flat cap had been doctored to alter the shape of the neb from a natural angle to a flat finish. I often wondered how he managed to see anything because his eyes were virtually covered. But he never missed anything. In another demonstration he produced a pair of his police boots which appeared to be patent leather, but the shine effect had been achieved by polishing alone. We were left in no doubt he expected our parade boots to look like his.

I knew ahead of time the boots needed special attention and a certain technique was needed to reach a high standard. My girlfriend Janette's grandfather, Frank Moore, was an ex-serviceman and knew some tricks to get the toe caps prepared to receive black polish and with a touch of spittle and a new yellow duster the shine emerged to a gloss like finish. All my colleagues were so proud of their boots that you made sure no one invaded your personal space where they could damage your footwear.

Every day we went to the parade square, forming into four classes of 25 officers. We were taught to march. It was very chaotic at first as many had never done it before, but the right practise makes perfect and Sergeant Foster soon knocked us into shape.

Classroom life was nine to five, with lunch and tea breaks. Our class instructor was Sergeant Maurice Ackroyd of Barnsley Borough Police. We were taught basic principles of English law, including crime and traffic matters. Every offence had a definition which had to be learned parrot fashion and we learned about a dozen definitions a day, being spot tested by the sergeant on a regular basis. We underwent two monthly examinations and a final examination covering all the course work. It was an arduous but very enjoyable three months, making new friends, building team work and gaining knowledge.

It was a great honour to be selected for the centre's soccer X1 to play other districts from the northern region and win the competition.

Following the final written examination, we had to wait a few days until the results were published on the main noticeboard in the quadrangle. It was announced the results were out and pandemonium broke out as our officers jostled to see their class position on the boards. I couldn't see my name anywhere and asked Sergeant Foster if he knew why. He checked my name badge and said, "Right, so you are Pc Newey of Rotherham. The reason is the top three students won't get theirs until the last day." I thought I'd done okay to get a top three position out of a hundred.

Preparations were being made for the final day's events at the course with the main attraction being

'The Passing Out Parade'. The seating was arranged to afford a grandstand view overlooking the parade square for the Commandant's march past. The main hall was all set for the family and friends of officers and to hear the Commandant's final address and presentation of prizes. There must have been an electricity power surge at the centre as irons were plugged in and were in constant use for hours as we pressed tunics and trousers to look our best for the parade.

The big day arrived which was quite an emotional experience in many ways. The marching formalities took place first with us all listening intently to Sergeant Foster's barked order to complete a flawless display, to great applause from the audience. Once we had marched out of sight, our cheers echoed all around and police helmets were thrown into the air in traditional fashion, followed by handshakes and back slapping.

We made our way to join our loved ones in the main hall and I had hold of Janette's hand on my left and my mother's on my right as the Commandant read out the final results in reverse order. It was a tense few minutes as third place went to a Nottinghamshire City Officer. I thought second would be okay – our hands squeezed tighter - Second place to a West Riding Officer. And top of the course; Pc6 Newey from Rotherham Borough Police. It was a great feeling I must admit and I proudly took the stage to receive a book prize of a Collins Dictionary.

I was naturally proud that my mother and Janette

were there to witness it, but I thought about my dad at that moment and was sure he'd be proud of me as well. I made sure I thanked Sergeant Ackroyd before I packed my kit and headed for home.

Chapter 4
Police Sports And Social

Rotherham Borough Police afforded you the opportunity to partake in a range of sporting disciplines including football, cricket, rugby, tennis and a range of other pastimes.

Following my return from training school, I met Pc Glyn Edwards, who was the force sports and social secretary and Captain of the football team.

The total manpower of the Borough Police was around 150, which included the Chief Constable and his senior command team. Many personnel being older or having no interest in participating in sport. This left the Superintendent with a nucleus of around fifteen men to select a team from.

The exigencies of duty, court attendance, annual leave and so forth, occasionally made it difficult to field a team, but we always did. The Borough were registered to play in the Yorkshire Police League, which included teams from neighbouring city and borough forces.

Barnsley Borough Police always provided a stiff test and had become a grudge fixture. They played their home games at The Queens Ground, the home of Barnsley Football Club.

I had met Bob Thompson and Peter Farnsworth at Pannal Ash and played representative football with them at the centre, but they were now playing for Barnsley and friendships counted for nothing.

My first game for Rotherham was at Barnsley and it was a testosterone fuelled event with 22 cops going at it hammers and tongs with no quarter given or asked. The beleaguered referee had his hands full trying to control some wild tackling, eventually calling both captains together to appeal for calm, as the laws of the game were in danger of being replaced by boxing's Marquess of Queensberry Rules.

Fighting and scuffles broke out as the game descended to new depths, leaving the referee with little alternative but to send everyone off and abandon the game. The formalities of handshakes and three cheers for your opponents were dispensed with, as pointless token gestures.

The national and local papers soon latched on to the news of this clash with unsavoury headlines about brawling bobbies in Barnsley bloodbath; a bit over the top, but nevertheless a headline grabber.

Our Chief Constable soon learned of the news and was furious, calling for our attendance in his office. He read us the riot act, stating if our actions had been committed out on the street, we'd have been locked up! Glyn's attempt to mitigate our position, claiming Barnsley were the aggressors was swiftly dismissed by our Chief, who told us in no uncertain terms, any future transgressions on the football field would have serious consequences with the dissolution of the football team. We knew it was no idle threat.

At that time police football had a notoriously bad reputation and only a few weeks later we were again involved in a bruising encounter away at Middlesbrough Police.

The Police Athletic Association, the umbrella organisation overseeing police sport, ran a national cup competition on the lines of the Football Association's world famous FA Cup. We had shocked a few people by reaching the 3rd round, having disposed of Dewsbury Borough and York City, but it seemed our days were numbered after being paired with the North East Middlesbrough outfit who were fancied to win the trophy. But we proved to be their nemesis and triumphed 2-1 despite one of their own officers refereeing the game. Undoubtedly the official favoured his mates, giving us nothing and them everything. He played at least 10 minutes injury time, giving them the opportunity to level or even win the tie. The game became fractious with books galore by both sides, but with a back three of Edwards, Hodgkinson and myself and six in midfield we held on for a famous victory. The Chief praised us and promulgated details of the win on the Force Daily Bulletin, along with other items of note.

Our cup win hit the buffers in the 4th round when we bowed out to a strong Leeds City team.

Our success was due to a great work ethic by the squad, which included Derek Kemp, Mick Curtis,

Barry Buncall, Terry Holroyd, Keith Hodgkinson, Glyn, myself, also the force enforcer, Dennis Thompson.

Glyn, never the one to miss any opportunity to protect our goals against column, recognised Sergeant Bob Brownrigg's son, John was a decent goalkeeper, although not a bobby, his name never attracted any scrutiny by officialdom. Although it was a minor deception, other teams practised it, taking the gamble of a fine or points deduction if caught. We never were.

We played our home game wherever we could find a pitch, usually on Corporation pitches, but local firms kindly allowed us to use their sports facilities, such as Robert Jenkins, Guest and Chrimes and Habershons.

I recall playing on Herringthorpe playing fields whose changing rooms afforded little or no security for personal belongings of participants, so one of the Borough team, Pc John Mugglestone tried to outwit the felons by putting a ten shilling note (pre decimal currency, worth 50p now) folded twice over into his football boot, underneath his stockinged heel. At the end of the game he removed his boot to discover the paper note had reduced to pulp due to the action of friction during the game. In the mid 1960's a constable's wage would have been about £10 per week, so ten shillings was a substantial loss, particularly when it involved a game of football.

Glyn and I as well as being good friends were keen tennis players. Growing up I played a lot of tennis at courts close to my home at nearby

Piccadilly. Some visionary had the inspiration to convert a disused quarry into a three tiered tennis facility of infinite beauty, with awesome flora and fauna; it was a joy to play there and pay the 3 shillings an hour fee (15p in today's money). If you didn't know, you'd swear Capability Brown, the 18th century landscape architect had been the creator.

Glyn decided to enter us into the PAA National Tennis Championships being held at the Ilkley Lawn Tennis and Squash club. We bought new kit, including new wooden racquets from Danny Williams Sports Shop in Rotherham. Danny was a former Rotherham player and knocked us a couple of quid off the bill.

The day arrived and we drove to Ilkley to discover a magnificent setting not quite Wimbledon, but close to it. The exquisitely manicured courts were superb. The event was of such a high standard; umpires, ball boys and new Slazenger white tennis balls were provided. In the locker room we had individual brass hooks with our nameplates on – Pc Newey/Pc Edwards, Rotherham Borough Police – Gentleman's Doubles Competitions.

The order of play was posted on a green baize noticeboard close by we saw our opponents were a pair from the Metropolitan Police. If my memory serves me right, I believe they were Pc Federer and Pc Nadal, for they proved to be just as good!

Glyn and I certainly looked the part, with 10 out of 10 for appearance, but scores plummeted after that in other departments, with a zero for skill! The match umpire shouted play and I did hear racquet on ball from the serves, but didn't see the ball, which was like an Exocet missile scorching the turf as it zipped by me at over 70mph. I thought maybe it was a fault, but my hopes were dashed when the umpire called, "15 Love." The coronation of our opponents deadly accurate serving soon racked up two sets at 6 – 0 6 – 0 and game over. We never heard, "Game to Newey and Edwards." The game was over in the time it took for short spin cycle on a Hotpoint washing machine.

The large crowd in the impressive stands applauded us as we trooped off the court, a gesture of sympathy we thought. I was hoping that no one had changed our name tags to, The Chuckle Brothers in the locker room, thankfully they hadn't. It was scant consolation to us that our opponents won the tournament. With game set and match against us, Glyn and I immediately decided to retire from competitive tennis.

I later learned the Piccadilly tennis courts had been subject to landfill, thus robbing the local community of a magnificent sporting venue and the vast revenue it could have generated.

Chapter 5
On The Beat

In early January 1966 I paraded at Rotherham Force HQ, and along with two other new recruits was marched into the office of the Chief Constable; Stanley William Morris. We stood to attention and saluted him before being told to stand easy by the duty sergeant in attendance.

Mr Morris perused our training school reports over his half-moon spectacles, periodically peering over them to look at us. My colleagues each received stern words from the chief, who suggested they should have worked harder. I was thinking that, as I'd won the book prize and come top of the course out of a hundred students, I was in for a glowing tribute for my hard work. I was standing proudly with my chest puffed out and was quickly brought down to earth when Mr Morris said, "Top of the course laddie. Well that counts for nothing because the hard work starts today. Off you all go". We all replied, "Thank you sir," saluted, and marched out of his office.

The three shift system operated days, afternoons and nights. It certainly played havoc with sleep patterns and my social life. I had become more accustomed to the wearing of the uniform with three months at training school under my belt, but the sanforized long sleeved shirt was very uncomfortable to wear being extra long - almost to knee length. The loose detachable collar fitted with studs front and back was so rigid it rubbed against your neck leaving red marks. The front stud played havoc with your Adam's apple, leaving a mark like a bullet hole; visible well into a long weekend off duty. It was a relief to disrobe at the end of a shift as the weight of heavy serge uniform, overcoat, boots, truncheon, handcuffs and helmet was very cumbersome, increasing greatly in inclement weather.

The in-house training particularly involving probationary constables was somewhat haphazard and is now so much more structured to ensure proper tuition by trained tutor constables. In the 1960's it was decided at the time of the shift briefing who you would accompany out on the beat. You might be lucky and be teamed with an enthusiastic officer or you might get someone who wasn't so keen to extend themselves. It seemed they'd reached mid service or beyond and were content to shake hands with door handles and do only as much as they had to.

There was so much to learn, systems and procedures to master. In the early days beat officers received direction and communication at shift briefings or via the station control room window. If you were out on patrol, the blue painted police pillar box contained a telephone and if you were needed the light would flash on top of the box.

Traffic patrol cars were equipped with fixed

radio so it was a little reminiscent of a jungle telegraph system as opposed to today's modern technology where every officer has state of the art personal telephones and GPS.

The main station operated six starting beat points. The town centre was obviously busiest, but did have a few downsides including point duty on days and afternoons at various bottlenecks affecting traffic flow.

The parade room had an area where white coats were stored for use on point. They were always starched and took an age to put on, as you had to force your hand down the sleeve and you walked around like the tin man until it had softened up. The dreaded point was outside the Essoldo Cinema on Corporation Street on the day shift as it was the preferred route for the Chief Constable to come to work in his diamond white Ford Zodiac, registration number 7777 ET. He lived off Moorgate and travelled down Ship Hill to his office, usually arriving by 08.30. Some of the more senior constables made him wait his turn in the queue, but if he was in a mood, he'd park his car and take over your point, waving his arms frantically and often causing utter chaos; gridlocking Westgate and Main Street. If Mr Morris deemed his delay was down to poor policeman-ship, bollockings were passed down to you via the chain of command to an Inspector and patrol sergeant.

The police HQ operated an amazing canteen, managed by three wonderful cooks, Edna, Kath and Jean, who provided cooked breakfasts, lunches and evening meals of top quality. The famous line attributed to Napoleon that an army marched on its stomach certainly applied here. The prisoners got the same grub as the officers, but when a jailer was delivering a breakfast to the cells, he'd likely encounter a hungry bobby en route and a sausage, a slice of bacon and a piece of fried bread would disappear from the plate before it was delivered! If you were on duty at one of the satellite mini stations known as boxes located at Ferham, Toll Bar, Greasbrough, Broom Valley and First Avenue, most officers took their own food, though tea-making facilities were available.

By February 1966 I was deemed able to be allowed out alone in the big wide world that was Rotherham Borough. It's quite strange to be a 19 year old in police uniform conferred with statutory and common law powers of arrest. It's quite daunting really.

My patrol sergeants were a bit one dimensional back then. I rarely got any practical advice other than to keep my nose clean and sit my promotion examination. Generally I would see one or the other once before a meal and again afterwards. They would decide a place name to book you by; entering the venue in their pocket note book. I would do the same with a corresponding time. Yet another archaic routine from bygone days.

Road accidents were a daily occurrence and a right royal pain to deal with, including non-injury bumps. They involved an inordinate amount of time; statement taking, booklet filling, box ticking and completing sketch plans. Sometimes weeks elapsed before a file could be submitted and often it was deemed to fall short of evidence needed to secure a successful prosecution. Eventually a higher power decreed that maybe millions of police man hours could be better used and we were working for the insurance companies. So 'knock for knock' was born and now police generally only became involved where it is an injury accident. This streamlining was years overdue.

With road accidents involving certain animals, generally dogs and cats, the officer attending the scene had a decision to make to decide the fate of the creature to prevent its continued suffering, as calling a veterinary surgeon out of hours would incur a cost to the taxpayer. The police control room carried a captive bolt gun which, with the authorising of the duty inspector, could be used for the humane killing of an animal. This instrument was simple to operate. Load, aim, fire to the centre of the animal's head, and it was over.

The RSPCA was situated at Erskine Road and contained kennels for the temporary homing of dogs and cages for cats. Another method of euthanizing smaller animals, normally feline, was a purpose made wooden box with a mesh inner grill and a top lid. The cat would be placed in the box, the meshed lid closed and covered with cotton wool padding, then copiously doused with chloroform. Health and safety rules weren't applicable then.

The top lid would be closed and latched, and after a few minutes the drug would normally kill the furry being, but there were occasionally mishaps! Thinking the job was done, I opened the lid and the cat shot out and through the open doors and into the night. I left the door open because of the chloroform fumes having a stupefying effect on humans too. Be unheard of in today's world. I accept these methods were primitive in the extreme, but thankfully custom and practice of the 1960's has been superseded by more humane methods.

Occasionally one of your prosecution files resulted in the defendant pleading not guilty to the offence alleged and it was necessary to give evidence using your pocket book to report the verbatim replies. My first experience of standing in the witness box was at Rotherham Magistrates' Court. but after a few times it became easier. The sweats and dry mouth used to come when you ascended the steps to stand beside the man in the red robe and wig at the old Assize and Quarter Sessions Court; now Crown Courts. The defence barristers, especially those with 'Q.C.' (Queens Counsel), after their name were masters of their craft. They were adept at assessing individuals as people and as witnesses. They were experienced at using rapier like questioning and probing in the right way to open up avenues, and then undermine and destroy even the most confident of people. I never underestimated any barrister, to give them any reason to undermine my professional credibility and a chance to degrade the case. The more witnesses involved in any case - police or civilian - was a bonus for the defence, giving them extra opportunity to exploit any weaknesses and increase their chance of producing an element of doubt in the minds of the jury. By knowing some barristers' methods and strategies, it gave you a slight advantage, in that you could coach your witness what to expect when they were pressurised. For a civilian, giving evidence is a stressful, nerve racking ordeal and you could only hope they didn't buckle under the immense strain.

I possessed a reasonably good retentive memory and with the knowledge I had acquired at training school, enhanced by two continuation courses during my two-year probationary period, I would have been so well equipped to sit the promotion examination to sergeant. I did so and passed, coming up in the top 100 in the country, qualifying me for the accelerated promotion scheme at Police College at Bramshill. After a paper sift and interviews I was rejected. I knew I was too young and lacked the experience needed.

Chapter 6
ABC

In any situation, including employment, it's paramount to master the basic principles to ensure your capabilities are maximised to the full. The police were rightly exposed when the Stephen Lawrence murder in London was shown time and again in numerous documentaries to have hopelessly failed to do the basics right, especially in the early stages. Millions of pounds were wasted going over old ground repeatedly, highlighting that the basics weren't done from the outset. When I went into CID in 1967 as a young detective, I was extremely fortunate to be mentored by Detective Constable Tony Scruby. He was a vastly experienced worldly-wise man and an extremely shrewd operator. Tony had informants in every area of the town and used them to garner vital information. If a housebreaking had been committed in the Borough, he'd have the culprit in custody and stolen property back in quick time. I hung onto his every word, watching his mannerisms and interviewing techniques; taking copies of his crime files and virtually shadowed his every move. Whilst we were the same rank, he was senior to me in service and wisdom. He helped me develop my personality and my confidence increased as I spent more time with him. I took on board all the advice he gave me. It was a great pleasure to go to work as my thirst for knowledge increased. Tony impressed upon me the dangers of complacency, highlighting a lesson he learned as a young officer: Following the arrest of a prisoner, he failed to search him and his captive pulled a knife, stabbing him in the face. He showed me the faint scar, which was a daily reminder of when he dropped his guard. First and foremost always protect yourself, use your handcuffs.

Another little pearl of wisdom were the letters, ABC.

A – accept nothing
B – believe nobody
C – challenge everything

This was never so true as when we attended a burglary at a house. The back door had been kicked in and the house ransacked. Uniform branch had got there first. After a cursory check told us the offender had fled the scene, Tony and I had a look around the place and we saw the table cloth twitch. Low and behold the criminal was in hiding under the table, clutching a bag of stolen property. Always expect the unexpected was his mantra.

The East Herringthorpe area of town had been blighted by a rash of house breaking offences, targeting cash and jewellery. Despite months of earnest observations by police, the offender continued his crime spree. In the early stages it wasn't clear how he was gaining entry or indeed leaving the crime. It was often thought that the complainant had misplaced their property, but the frequency of the crimes indicated a pattern; a definite MO (Modus Operandi) and eventually it became clear that all the houses being attacked had mortice locks fitted to their doors. These operated by the larger type key, often 4 inches long. The offender was easily able to see if any such key was in the lock and had perfected the simple technique of using long nosed pliers to grip the end of the metal key, turning it to unlock the door and once inside steal what he wanted. He relocked the door using the reverse procedure. This epidemic of criminality netted the burglar thousands of pounds and he clearly needed to be caught - and soon.

A stroke of good fortune resulted in an alert member of the public observing a man in dark clothing casing a neighbour's house, who he knew to be on holiday. He was aware of the spate of crime in his area and bravely confronted the man, detaining him until police arrived. Christopher Pinehurst, aged 35, was in custody and brought to Frederick Street police station. Effectively he had been arrested on a "wing and a prayer". No apparent offence had been committed. He was saying absolutely nothing. I was the control room/custody sergeant responsible to receive and document prisoners when Pc Carter escorted Pinehurst into the Charge Office where I was seated at a desk. Being a confirmed people-watcher and professionally curious, I noted his gait seemed somewhat awkward as he walked towards me, as though his ankles were shackled. Once I had completed the booking in process, I searched him to discover a few coins in his hip pockets and a comb in his back pocket. He hadn't any medical issues especially affecting his ability to walk. I decided there and then to strip search him. He reluctantly dropped his trousers to expose his Y fronts. I said, "Right, don't be shy, drop them too". He did so and in a spilt second gravity occurred when a pair of long nosed pliers hit the cold concrete floor.

I said, "Well, well, we've been looking for you a long time".

He looked shell shocked that his cunning concealment had been discovered. Had it not, he would likely have gone into the main cell area and taken his pick from a number of places to dispose of the pliers, the vital evidence would have been lost forever and he could have invoked his right to silence, and without any evidence would have been released and the offences may have never been detected. As it was, Pinehurst admitted five specimen charges of burglary dwelling, asking for 120 similar offences to be taken into consideration and he was jailed for 5 years. No property was ever recovered. Pc Carter and myself received commendations. I dedicated mine to Tony Scruby, for without his advice, I may never have had the presence of mind to conduct that search.

I didn't think I had done anything ultra special in this case, it was simply a case of heightening my sense of awareness at a particular time and place.

In 1989, shortly after the horrific events of

Hillsborough, Tony passed away. It was an honour and privilege to be a pallbearer for his final journey. RIP to my dear friend and mentor and thank you for your guidance. I owe him so much.

Chapter 7
My First Post Mortem

In February 1966 I paraded for duty on afternoons at Ferham Police Box, which was a mini police station on the outskirts of town, where three officers covered different beats on a 24 hour cycle. The desk in the office carried IN/OUT trays for reports, mail and such like. My beat covered Ferham Road public mortuary and I saw an envelope in the tray marked, "By hand, Roy Williams". I walked the few yards to the morgue, envelope in hand. I rang the bell and Roy Williams, the mortuary attendant opened the door. He was about 30 years old, 5 foot 7 inches tall and bespectacled. I immediately noticed his unblemished face; in fact it was wax like, similar to a model at Madam Tussaud's establishment. He invited me inside as I handed him the envelope, which he opened and removed some papers he'd been expecting. Roy said, "You're new, eh? First visit?"

I said, "Yes, new and first time."

I was struck by the layout of the room, which was spotlessly clean and almost every fitting was stainless steel. It had three stainless steel tables in the centre of the room, which I learned was where the bodies were dissected. Roy had a small office just off the main room and he directed me to one of four chairs in the room, where I sat down. He said, "I think it's tea time, you fancy a cuppa?" as he picked up a Hotpoint stainless steel kettle and filled it with water from a sink tap. I accepted and said, "Please, I'll have a coffee, just milk, no sugar". He measured a spoonful of coffee into each of two mugs and walked a few paces to a row of huge floor to ceiling refrigerators, opening one and exposing a vertical row of six corpses, all with tags on their right toe. I was momentarily taken aback at this sight. Roy bent down and picked up a pint of milk from the fridge floor, he closed the door and walked back to where the coffee mugs were sitting on a table. He removed the silver top, looked at me and said, "Say when". I just blurted out before he poured the milk, "No, no. I don't have milk, thanks, just remembered". Roy poured milk into his mug. I thought 'How can he drink his coffee when the milk has been in with the corpses?'

Moments later the main door opened and in came Professor Alan Usher, who was one of Britain's leading forensic pathologists. He was the archetypal Home Office Pathologist and also the senior Police Surgeon to the police. He completed over 1000 post mortems annually and had taken part in over 800 murder investigations in his career. He was a rotund man about 5 foot 8 inches; always wearing his trademark gold rimmed half-moon glasses and a three piece black suit. He looked like a doctor should look. He was immensely popular with police officers, always going to great lengths to explain and demonstrate his findings, even to the newest recruit. He was a premier league standard professor of great wit and wisdom, as well as a brilliant after dinner speaker, enjoying national fame. A truly remarkable man of exceptional ability only a very few could hope to match.

Prof. Usher, as he liked to be called said, "Okay then Roy, what's new and who is this young man? Not seen him before". Roy handed him a wad of papers needing his signature, and said, "This is Pc Newey, boss, he's a new recruit". I stood up as the professor offered his hand for me to shake. It was like a wrestler's grip. As we made eye contact, Prof Usher said, "Very pleased to meet you, Pc Newey.".

"Likewise, sir," I replied.

Prof. Usher trusted Roy, having taught him to dissect a body to a high standard and prepare the organs, brain and other body parts for his final inspection, before signing off the papers and completing death certificates. Murder cases were the exclusive domain of Professor Usher. He did everything himself from start to finish and was totally prepared should he be called into the witness box at any future trial.

Some years later I saw him perform three post mortems involving murder victims. He was the consummate professional at the top of his game. He coined a phrase on his after dinner

circuit speeches, "I'm often called an expert; well an ex is a has been and a spurt is a drip under pressure. It always received a rapturous response from the audience.

I bid Roy and Prof. Usher a good afternoon, telling them I had my beat to cover and as I was leaving, the Prof. said, "You'll have to come to one of my PM's." I thanked him and said I would do and it was three weeks before I saw him at work. I was on mornings and had just had a full English breakfast in the police canteen, when Sergeant Frank Scott dropped his hand on my shoulder and said, "Come on lad, we've a post mortem to attend. Prof. Usher is doing the carvery today!". We went to Ferham Mortuary to witness Prof Usher donning his rubber gloves and white apron Roy Williams laid out the instruments that would be required. The master surgeon made his first incision near to the throat of the elderly man's corpse and drew the razor sharp blade down to his naval. This released bodily gases and fluids. The acrid smell immediately entered my airways, causing a nauseous reaction, causing me to rush to the sink. My breakfast didn't taste the same coming back!! I felt ghastly. Sgt. Scott was laughing, but Prof. Usher was quite sympathetic, suggesting I tried some breathing techniques when I attended another PM. I'm sure I'd been set up by my sergeant to eat a hearty breakfast ahead of the event, which after a half a century still resides in my psyche.

Prof Usher saw me at West Yorkshire Police Academy Detective Training School in 1971, where he gave a lecture. He remembered my debut at the morgue, enquiring if I had recovered from the experience. I smiled and nodded that I had.

Sadly the great man died in 1998 aged 68. I often wondered if he had escaped the mortuary slab and got a friend in his field to sign him a Death Certificate to obviate a PM being performed.

In the late 1960's, Roy Williams was allowed to have an assistant to help out with the cleaning tasks at the morgue. It transpired his helper only worked on a part time basis for a bit of pin-money. He and his wife had their own thriving business on the outskirts of town – it was a butchers shop!! The news soon got out and the fertile, sometimes cynical minds of some constabulary members thought the morgue man might be selling the viscera, heart, kidney and livers of some of the post mortem subjects in his meat market. There was an old saying, "You ought to change your butcher."
I know the wives of some policemen actually did!

Chapter 8
The Las Vegas Of The North

In the mid 1960's and well into the next decade, South Yorkshire came to be known by many as The Las Vegas Of The North, for its entertainment scene and its popular nightclub venues. Big pay days were on offer to entice the showbiz superstars of the day to venture North from the bright lights of London. One of the forerunners was a small village establishment called Greasbrough Working Men's Club, which was suddenly catapulted to national notice. Some of the biggest names in showbiz played there, including: Lulu, Tom Jones and Bob Monkhouse. Even Jayne Mansfield, the blonde American actress, visited the club. Rotherham also had The Tivoli and the Oasis nightclubs, although these were slightly smaller venues, and attracted a different clientele.

The Brecon Hotel on Moorgate, was owned by Athol Carr, and he had many connections in the showbiz industry and an "A" list of celebs would stay there when they were appearing in the region, with the likes of Billy Connolly, Roy Castle, Vince Hill, Paul Daniels, Matt Monroe and Michael Parkinson among the guests. These stars felt comfortable staying with the Carr's and could relax ahead of show time, then return for a quiet drink later, away from prying eyes. The Brecon was a residential establishment, where the existing licensing regulations allowed bona-fide hotel guests to use the bar facilities after the end of normal permitted hours. As operational CID Officers, we would call into the hotel to ensure everything was in order - at least that was our excuse!

A good friend of Athol's was off duty Pc David Caro, who was relaxing in the bar when we dropped by. Around 1 am the night bell rang and Athol asked David to answer it. He came back saying, "It's a Scotsman called Billy Connolly and he says he's staying here. Likely tale, I told him to get lost".

We were all doubled up laughing, as Athol shot to the door, telling David, "He is staying here, it's Billy Connolly, the comedian". Caro was oblivious to who he was. 'The Big Yin' was not impressed and unloaded a torrent of abuse upon David.

In the vent of major crime in the borough area, officers would be deployed to strategic positions to intercept/detain fleeing suspects. A jewellers had been robbed in the town centre and I was a CID man accompanying a traffic officer called Pc Alan Angel in his blue Ford Zephyr. We were directed to an area called Greasbrough Tops to keep observation, when moments later an American-registered Chevrolet Impala zoomed by at a rate of knots.

Pc Angel said, "Bloody hell, he's doing 90."
It was a 30 miles per hour limit and we gave chase using the blues and twos, before stopping the car on Potter Hill.

I knew the driver, but Alan didn't and he started to talk to him about his speeding offence, telling him he could be jailed for his attempt at low flying in a car! The driver looked shaken and asked if he could make amends, so I said, "Well Mr P.J. Proby, there may well be a way out. (P.J. Proby was an American rock star out of the Elvis Presley mould and famous for his skin tight trousers, which would frequently split during his act, enjoyed by his screaming female followers). I asked if he was appearing at Greasbrough Club, he said he was and immediately offered to supply free tickets for any constabulary members who wanted to see the show. He duly left us 20 tickets on the door. He was advised about his speed on British roads. No further action was taken.

In the 1970's, Sheffield University students held a "Rag Week" consisting of various fund raising events for the benefit of local charities. They produced a magazine called, "The Twicker" which was always a sell out publication, again for good causes.

In 1976 the popular TV show host and DJ, Noel Edmonds was staying in Rotherham at The Brecon, whilst appearing in the area. One of the university organising committee sensibly notified the police of their intention to "kidnap" the star as a charity publicity stunt to raise funds by getting a ransom paid by the highest bidder. The press were in on the story, but there was on drawback; Noel wasn't at all keen to be involved. I went to see him at his hotel and explained the situation. He was absolutely horrified at the prospect of the kidnap plot. He was scheduled to leave the day after, going to London by train from Sheffield. He demanded we protect him and we devised a plan to handcuff him to me and put him on the train to thwart the students.

It was definitely a 'No Deal' for Noel.

Chapter 9
Amalgamation

Rotherham Borough Police and Sheffield City Police combined in 1967 to become Sheffield and Rotherham Constabulary, and the Borough became known as G Division. All the Borough constables and sergeants had to relinquish their collar numbers and be reassigned with new ones starting from 900 and rising depending on seniority of service. Some officers viewed the amalgamation as a takeover, with numerous supervisory ranked officers moving to Rotherham into uniform and CID roles. I was in CID at that time and still had an old Borough Detective Sergeant heading my team. He was Robert Walker; a huge man who always wore a brown gaberdine mackintosh and his trademark trilby. He was definitely "old school" and was very well respected by staff and criminals alike. His local knowledge was second to none and whilst his paperwork wasn't the best, he made up for it in other areas. I would often go out on patrol in a plain car, sit outside scrap yards, licensed premises and suchlike, looking for criminals and garnering intelligence. There was always something going on. Bob's sense of humour was very dry. On one occasion the radio crackled into life with the control room asking for CID to respond.

"CID, can you rendezvous with Pc 999 Hill and Pc 1001 Caro in All Saints Square? They need advice." I acknowledged we'd attend, then, after a moment's thought, DS Walker quipped, "Ah, Pc 999 and Pc 1001. Urgent and detergent". I later told the office staff that Bob had uttered this immortal line, which is still remembered half a century on.

G Division CID had four teams of four made up of a Detective Sgt. and three Detectives, with a Detective Chief Inspector in overall charge. He was a Sheffield City man called John Naylor; a dour insensitive man obsessed with statistics, which was the Home Office's yardstick of measuring performance levels at national force and divisional levels. Each detective had their own book, showing every crime they had been allocated and its status and disposal. Informants were always a useful asset to any investigators on their quest to detect crime. "Snouts" as they were known, came in various forms, but invariably the bottom line was to earn some tax free beer money and it proved there was no honour amongst thieves. Occasionally it was decided not to prosecute every criminal for every crime as common sense and discretion could be applied. If the circumstances were right, you could enlist the services of the person as a tool in the battle against crime as an informant. Periodically it was a useful police ploy to play one informant off against another to get the real truth of the matter, always handy if you held all the aces. Good to be ahead of the game.

A young lady who lived on Westgate in town had received a substantial cash payout from an insurance company as compensation following a brain injury she had sustained in a car accident. She owned a cake making shop and was very generous with her windfall, clearly not cash prudent due to the adverse effects of her accident. The criminal fraternity quickly took full advantage of her vulnerability, with two local crooks the main culprits. She was fleeced out of hundreds of pounds by these two alone. She was being blackmailed, and, convinced they had confidential information about her, she freely handed over more cash. Eventually an informant came forward to expose the scam, resulting in Det. Sgt. Swift and DC Storr being deputed to conduct an investigation into the claims. In those days police interviews were subject to much scrutiny by lawyers. The system was far from perfect as interviews took place and the officers involved didn't record them into their official pocket note until later. The rules of evidence made the notes admissible when officers told the court the notes were made at the first available opportunity. Lawyers and barristers always took an opportunity to challenge the integrity and validity. Often alleging their client had been 'verballed', jargon for fabricating evidence, or manufacturing replies admitting, or implicating themselves in, the offence. Over time the system in place today using taped interviewing was introduced nationwide, ensuring absolute integrity and total fairness to the accused.

DC Storr tried to outsmart the judge by

explaining he hadn't sufficient writing materials to do as he suggested. The judge retorted, "Then why didn't you use your official pocket book to do it?" The CID officers' pocket book was roughly the size of a regular paperback novel, and half as thick. It was usually kept in the officer's desk drawer and not carried anywhere. DC Storr, thinking he would stop the judge's persistence, flippantly replied, "CID men don't carry their pocket books, your honour". Inviting the judge to ask, "Why not?"

DC Storr, "The shape of the book spoils the cut of my suit."

The bewigged judge slowly shook his head in dismay as muted laughter broke out in the courtroom, particularly amongst the press corps. Despite all this, convictions were secured and jail time resulted for the offenders. The press and cartoonists in particular had an absolute field day as many tabloids exploited the opportunity to deride the detective's unguarded quip to the judge by showing police officers carrying a ladies' shoulder bag to carry their pocket note books.

Even the Police Review, the police's own publication, saw the funny side, with an article about it.

Chapter 10
The Dalton Gang

Any aficionado of the old American West in the late 1800's will have heard of The Dalton Gang and remember them as a band of outlaws. Well this isn't about them, but a gang of five outlaws based in Dalton, near Rotherham.

In the late 1960's this team were virtually full time criminals operating in the region, specialising in the theft of high value metals of any shape and size. They accessed equipment which enabled them to cut anything down to size for ease of transportation and dispose of it to any of the many scrap dealers in the area to realise a cash payment. So often they provided false details and few questions were asked of them. Criminals will steal anything and everything and go anywhere, if it is portable, saleable and doable, then they will steal it.

The nationally famous brand, 'KP Nuts' had a factory based on the Eastwood Trading Estate in Rotherham. Their transport fleet, and advertising logo was "Britain's Favourite Nut". They processed peanuts and had a facility to roast them on an industrial scale, with the cutting edge technology they possessed. Part of the production process included the use of enormous copper vats shaped like giant onions. These vats were very expensive to fabricate and they had a limited lifespan before it was necessary to replace them with new stock. The expired vats were left within the factory compound to await collection and disposal. The Achilles heel of the company lay at the rear of the premises. The front and sides had high metal fencing, but none at the back, as the embankment sloped away down to the River Don and was only accessible by waterborne craft. The copper vats could be seen from across the river by anyone walking its path. The Foljambe Public House, situated close to Dalton, was the preferred meeting place for the gang to plot their next crime and the vats soon came onto their agenda. They knew copper was a valuable commodity and these two vats would fetch a handsome price on the weight scales. They knew the only way they could get them was by crossing the river.

Most criminal groups have associates outside their own circle, a bit like a criminals co-operative society. They exchange information and equipment, vehicles etc., on a loan or hire basis and come to a financial arrangement that benefits all concerned. Detective Sergeant Bob Walker had a confidential informant who had never failed him with his accurate details of where, when and how a crime would go down. The criminals had acquired two small rowing boats and planned to transport them to the opposite side of the river bank and paddle across to reach the KP factory side. They proposed to drag a copper container to the water and position it in between their boats and paddle downriver to the far side, pull it up to road level, load it onto a flat back lorry, then go back for the second, and load that one in identical fashion. We were certain the sergeant's source was a bona fide informant and not acting as an Agent provocateur, whereby the person was being paid by the police to provoke the suspects to commit illegal acts. The well-informed police source assured us he wasn't involved in the conspiracy and had gleaned his inside knowledge by his well-honed eavesdropping ability. He was left in no doubt that if he was being untruthful to us, he wouldn't be paid for his information. We knew days in advance when the gang would strike and details of the vehicles involved. The police plan was carefully laid, the trap was set for a 1 am Sunday start and they were bang on time. We had officers positioned at strategic points with road exits covered. The noose was tightening.

Over the next three hours or so, the gang were seen to carry out their plan, working harder than the resident beavers who inhabited the riverbank. The reason we didn't intervene to effect arrests in the initial stages was the risk of the river and the darkness and the antecedent history of the gang. We knew they wouldn't surrender without using violence in order to escape; it was to prove an excellent strategy, as they expended so much energy to drag the containers to the water and paddle their boats, gradually exhausting themselves. Once the second copper container was aboard the lorry we struck, with shouts of, "POLICE, POLICE."

Torches were trained on all the five men. They offered no resistance, they were spent; they sunk to their knees as handcuffs were applied. Now the game was up, a bit of light hearted banter took place between the felons and the captors. They clearly suspected their arrests hadn't happened by chance and wanted to know who had tipped us off. We told them nothing.

They all received terms of imprisonment, maybe telling the prison chef they were all allergic to nuts.

Chapter 11
Match Of The Day

It was always an enjoyable experience performing match day duty at the ground of my special club, Rotherham United.

On Saturday 21st March 1982 Rotherham United hosted Queens Park Rangers. The West London outfit were managed by former England boss, Terry Venables, whose dugout team included, Tony Currie and physio, Jock Skinner.

Emlyn Hughes, the ex Liverpool and England legend was the player/manager of Rotherham. His assistant was Barry Claxton, who also performed physiotherapy duties. Meaning Barry was outnumbered five to one in the pitch-side dugouts.

Emlyn and his staff were always very accommodating to the local police, allowing them the use of the clubs gymnasium, where the Police Support Unit Officers trained and maintained their fitness levels.

The game against QPR was very competitive, involving two teams seeking promotion. John Seaman scored for Rotherham at The Tivoli end, after only a few minutes and it proved to be the games only goal.

Several personal battles developed with Emlyn and Terry Fenwick clashing. Fenwick was sent off for elbowing his opponent in the face.

I was duty sergeant for this fixture, responsible for the supervision of the perimeter track and I was soon having to intervene in touchline altercation after Rotherham's bellicose midfielder, Gerry Gow committed a foul which incensed the QPR bench. Five of them were in conflict with Barry Claxton, it was 'handbags' really – a football term used when posturing takes place and where no actual violence occurs but looks worse than it is. I was positioned near the tunnel a good few yards away from the action. The Match Commander had claimed to have witnessed the scuffling and believed Claxton was the cause of it. He told me to arrest him for public order offence. I was faced with a dilemma as Claxton had treated me for an injury just days before. As I marched purposefully towards the scene, I pondered my options and decided firstly to restore order to allow the game to resume. I told Barry Claxton to calm down and sit down. He was blaming his opposite number, Jock Skinner for the fracas. I was conscious that Yorkshire Television were covering the game with sports commentator, John Helm describing the live action to millions of viewers. I had observed boom microphones positioned around track-side, so I was aware of their acute sound pickup capability. Skinner was testing my patience and I had to issue a strong ultimatum with a caveat of arrest attached to it. I said, "If you don't sit down dickhead, I'll lock you all up." Tony Currie eventually bundled him into the dugout. I remained there to keep the peace. I pretended to issue a finger wagging lecture to Barry to give them the impression of my impartiality.

Another Rangers player was dismissed for a tackle on John Breckin before Ronnie Moore got first use of the soap for Rotherham with a late tackle on their keeper. So it was 10 to 9 in bodies and a one nil victory.

At the post match press conference, Emlyn whispered to me, "Hey, John, thanks for looking after Barry," followed by a cheeky wink.

John Piper was the sports writer for The Sheffield Telegraph and Star, also covering The Green 'un sports paper. He was a gentleman and few knew he saw active service in World War 2 as an RAF Officer. John approached me keen to learn about my conversation with both dugouts. I gave him the unabridged version. He smiled, raising his eyebrows! In his newspaper column he reported, "Sgt John Newey arrived at the scene with discreet advise for all." Very succinctly put, I thought.

It was a game where Ray Mountford added another clean sheet to his impressive record of shut outs which he reminds me of on our curry nights out. Ray later served in the South Yorkshire Police as an Inspector.

Out of all the police foot-beats operating in the borough, my absolute favourite was the Masborough beat. It was like a small town within a town. So much to do, so much going on. The local residents and business people loved to see a bobby on the beat.

I enjoyed the interaction with them, making many friends along the way, including Mario Kasic, whose immigrant parents ran a general store on Masborough Street. Mario often acted as their interpretor as they came to terms with the Yorkshire dialect.

Thriving businesses operated there. Walter Moore's Pork Butches, The Sarsaparilla shop, Rushton's Locksmiths, Heatons Bath Works, along with the Kasics all provided an endless supply of tea and biscuits for the beat officers.

There were pubs every few yards, Moulders Rest, Travellers Rest, Golden Cup, Royal Standard, Millmoor Hotel, Queens, College, Phoenix, Butchers, Carters Rest, Little Station, all now gone, with only three surviving from that era - Prince Of Wales, New Inn and The Midland. Wonderful memories.

Mentioning Rotherham United, it would be remiss of me not to mention Derek Dalton, polio victim since the age of two and a legend in the town. He won "The People" newspaper Superfan award. I met him in 1971 after the Millers earned an FA Cup replay at Leeds United after drawing at home. There was no disability legislation in place then, but I knew some Leeds officers who ensured a place for Derek at Elland Road. I later drove my dear friend, Derek to grounds all over England and Wales to watch his beloved team. He was an outstanding man of great wit, knowledge and humility. We met Pelé, Eusebio, Stanley Matthews and many more and Derek even met The Queen on her visit to Rotherham. This extraordinary man was officially remembered with a fitting tribute in the form of a blue plaque dedicated to his memory and mounted on a wall at The New York Stadium, the home of his beloved club.

Derek's name is synonymous with the club and if you'd had the privilege of meeting or knowing him, you were very fortunate indeed.

RIP Del Boy, you'll never be forgotten.

"Up The Millers."

Chapter 12
Pc 251 Frank Phillips

In 1981 I was a sergeant in the Sheffield and Rotherham Constabulary at G Division, Frederick Street, Rotherham. My responsibilities included supervising the area constables who policed the sub division. Their duties included a myriad of tasks; the execution of warrants, service of summonses and foreign force enquiries. This body of officers could also be utilised at short notice anywhere in the force area for manpower-intensive duties such as murder enquiries, public order situations and football matches.

Pc Phillips had joined the Sheffield City police in the late 1950's, serving as a foot patrol officer in the steel city until matrimonial issues caused the Personnel Department to transfer him to G Division; he would have no involvement in the final decision. I remember him parading for duty looking somewhat forlorn in his new surroundings. He had a brief interview with the Divisional Commander who went through the usual formalities, before he came to the Area Office, as it was known. I introduced myself to him and asked him to give me a résumé of his career, which he did. He openly admitted the breakdown of his marriage had hit him very hard, but said he was determined to rebuild his life and was looking forward to the new challenge at Rotherham. He disclosed that paperwork wasn't his best asset, but promised he'd always give 100%. I told Frank we had proposed to install him as the new regular town centre beat officer. This was designed to keep him under review, especially from a welfare perspective. Pc Phillips was a down to earth, no nonsense officer, totally genuine and hard-working. True to his word he soon got to grips with town centre life and displayed zero tolerance to drunks or public disorder in any shape or form. He was the quintessential old style copper that shop keepers in particular loved having around town. They wanted reassurance and he provided it.

Unsolicited letters of appreciation were often received at the police station, complimenting the officer's work in keeping order in the town. I would occasionally join him on foot patrol on his patch and observe people afford him great respect.

"Hello Pc Phillips." "Nice to see you officer." they would comment.

It was nice to see that he'd integrated well into his new surroundings and was overcoming his personal difficulties; Frank would often remark he was benefiting from his transfer and was enjoying his life. One day, out of the blue, he announced he had booked a table at a nice restaurant in Sheffield and he invited the Superintendent and his Area Supervisors and their wives to join him for dinner, such was his gratitude to all of us for guiding him in his hour of need. It was a wonderful gesture by a very genuine man. We accepted without hesitation.

As time went by, Frank was now a respected member of the group. I ran a holiday idea by him, suggesting my travel agent friend could arrange a trip to Pattaya in Thailand and maybe he'd enjoy a sunshine vacation. Frank checked his annual leave allocation, submitted his application form and his trip was booked the very next day.

John Newey

Photographs

John's mother & father and grandmother

John Newey

The Author aged 5

Rotherham United Football Club Limited
Season 1961 – 62

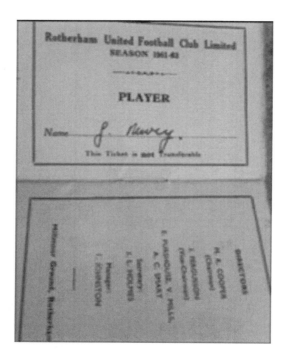

John Newey

COUNTY BOROUGH OF ROTHERHAM

Chief Constable's Office,

S. W. MORRIS
CHIEF CONSTABLE

TELEPHONE
NO. 4342

Ref. BB/BP.Admin

Rotherham.

P.O. BOX 1.

6th September, 1965

Dear Sir,

      With reference to your application for
appointment as a Constable in this Force, I shall
be glad if you will attend the Surgery of
Dr. H. H. Smith, Dale House, Dale Road, Rawmarsh,
at 7 p.m. on Wednesday, 8th September, 1965, for
the purpose of a medical examination.

      Please take with you a sample of your
urine.

      Yours faithfully,

                       Chief Constable.

Mr. J. W. Newey,
71, Brookfield Avenue,
Swinton,
Mexborough,
Yorks.

ALL COMMUNICATIONS TO BE ADDRESSED TO THE CHIEF CONSTABLE

County Borough of Rotherham

TELEPHONE NOS. 4243 (3 lines)

THE CHIEF CONSTABLE
ROTHERHAM

EB/BF.Admin

Your Ref. No.

S. W. MORRIS
CHIEF CONSTABLE

Chief Constable's Office,

Rotherham.

P.O. BOX 1.

24th September, 1965

Dear Sir,

With reference to your application for appointment as a constable in this Force, I am prepared to offer you an appointment and shall be glad to receive confirmation that you wish to accept this.

Subject to your acceptance, you will be required to report at these Headquarters at 9 a.m. on Monday, 11th October, 1965, prior to attending a course of instruction at the Police Training Centre, Pannal Ash, Harrogate, which commences on Monday, 18th October, 1965. When you report for duty on the 11th October, 1965, please bring with you your National Insurance Card and Income Tax form P45.

I shall be glad if you will call at these Headquarters in the near future in order that you may be fitted out with uniform.

Yours faithfully,

Superintendent & D.C.C.
for Chief Constable.

Mr. J. W. Newey,
71, Brookfield Avenue,
Swinton,
Mexborough,
Yorks.

John Newey

Pc 6 Newey September 1965

**Pc 6 John Newey
Rotherham Borough Police at Number 3 Police
District Training Centre, Pannal Ash, Harrogate
1965
Back row 2nd in from right**

Number 3 Police District Training Centre
Representative Soccer X1

John Newey front row 2nd in from right

Last photo of RBP
21/4/1967

John Newey

Detective Constable John Newey
Rotherham CID
1968

John Newey

West Yorkshire Police Academy Inspectors Course 1986

Inspector John Newey back row 3rd in from right

**Mass Murderer Anthony Arkwright After
Remand At Rotherham Magistrates Court
Arkwright, Left, Spiked Hair
Stephen Smith, Lawyer, Back
Inspector Newey, First Police After Smith**

John Newey

**Inspector John Newey SYP in 1988
At a Wath Against Chemicals Rally On A
Freezing Cold Day**

John Newey

TELEPHONE:
SHEFFIELD (0742) 768522
TELEX: 547996
FAX: (0742) 523243

R B WELLS QPM MA
CHIEF CONSTABLE

SOUTH YORKSHIRE POLICE
POLICE HEADQUARTERS
SNIG HILL
SHEFFIELD S3 8LY

7 October 1991

Inspector J Newey
C2 Sub-Division

Dear John,

I wanted to record my appreciation of the work that you did in dealing with the pit bull terrier at Thrybergh last week. Inevitably there will be cries of "cruelty" by some who do not appreciate the ferocity of the animal and who fail short of dealing, daily, with the realities of life.

This letter is to reassure you both - insofar that it is necessary - that I support your action and admire you for it. In a past command, I have authorised the use of fire extinguishers to cope with the same menace but the looped noose was, under the circumstances, a legitimate device.

I do hope that you have both recovered from the ordeal. You will be as sorry as I was that a creature has lost its life but it is difficult to see how it might have been otherwise.

With kind regards

Richard Wells

85

**Inspector Newey 2/10/91 with snare that killed
American Pit Bull Terrier**

John Newey Receiving Long Service and Good Conduct Medal in 1991 From The Lord Lieutenant Of The County

Pelé, Derek Dalton & myself

Chapter 13
Simply Classical

In the late 1960's football, match violence was beginning to cause problems for police forces throughout the UK, although Rotherham United had some success in containing it. The configuration of the old Millmoor Stadium made it quite easy to police, with away supporters arriving by coach being directed to the railway end secure parking. Trains arriving at the old Masbrough station allowed police to shepherd supporters across Masbrough Street to the railway end stand, via Millmoor Lane.

Rotherham United had a handful of unruly youths who saw match days as their opportunity to cause aggravation and disorder by lying in wait to waylay visiting fans. My colleague, Steve Morton, and myself were on CID patrol before and after a home game, acting as "spotters" for trouble makers. We had identified a skinhead youth aged about 18, wearing a white T-shirt, powder blue jeans, mid brown Doc Marten boots, the "uniform" of a bovver boy of the day. We observed him shouting obscenities at the away fans being escorted towards the station. He then made threats towards them and was on the verge of attacking them, when we intervened. We put him into the back seat of the CID car, with his feet either side of the transmission tunnel. We challenged him about his presence there and about his aggressive threatening behaviour. He claimed he was en-route home, which was in a totally different direction. The police radio system of the day was a 2 piece PYE pocket phone, a transmitter, and a receiver. I was in the passenger seat and asked police control for an electoral roll check of our detainee. I asked the skinhead his name, he replied "Tchaikovsky".

My colleague immediately thought our man was being flippant in the extreme. In a flash, DC Morton reached between the seats, bringing both their sets of eyebrows into direct contact.

He said forcefully, "Don't take the piss."

"I'm not. Honest. It's my name. Honest it is." he said, as he tried to reassure the officer he wasn't lying.

DC Morton said, "You're in enough bother, don't make it worse by telling me you're a fucking composer".

The police PYE receiver called me with my electoral roll enquiry, saying, "Far Lane address shows family of three, all named TCHAIKOVSKY!"

DC Morton and myself exchanged a knowing glance and had to accept his honesty, which was confirmed with his driving licence which he was carrying with him. The skinhead was given a stern warning about his actions and advised about his future conduct. "One Shot" Polaroid cameras were available to us and we took a mugshot of the youth and showed it to him. I said it would be shown to all the officers working football duty and he was a marked man. He apologised and went on his way.

Chapter 14
£1,000,000 Heist

We finally convinced Pc Phillips a Far East holiday would do him the world of good. He jetted off to Thailand from Manchester airport. We had access to his Ford Escort car which was coming up to its 10th birthday and was really showing its age. At an Area Constables Meeting at Frederick Street Police Station, it was agreed we would all donate a pound each to enable Frank's car to have a respray and makeover. "Ronnie's Paint Shop" at Clifton, Rotherham was selected to carry out the job. The proprietor always did good work and looked after policemen with a good discount. The collection had reached £30 which in 1982 was a decent amount and Ronnie told us he would provide an all-in service, plus the paint job for the thirty quid.

At G Division DHQ I was in the Area Office with Pc Nev Edwards, one of the area officers, when Ronnie called to advise that the car was ready for collection. So we acquired a spare CID car to go to collect it. Frank's car was stunning and was in showroom condition. The tyres had even been blackened. We were sure Frank would love his resprayed car. En route back to Rotherham DHQ we needed to call into an insurance office on Fitzwilliam

Road, to collect some statements. We drove in two cars, exercising extreme care, as you would, to ensure Frank's car went unscathed. We parked on some spare ground requiring us to walk 150 yards to the offices.

A line of cars was parked on Shakespeare Road to our left, and a few yards ahead of us I could see an old Vauxhall saloon with two men in the front. Slowing our walk down to nothing, I had a better view of the car and the men. Nev was on my inside and I beckoned with my hand to move in behind me and we reduced our speech to hushed tones. I said to Nev, "These two look a bit suspect". The men carried on with what they were doing, completely oblivious to us. By wearing our civilian coats we weren't as obvious as policemen in full uniform. The driver had wedged a portable typewriter between his chest and the steering wheel and was typing onto bankers cheque sized pieces of paper, which his mate was passing over to him from a perspex wallet. I was intrigued to see a plastic Johnson's talcum powder container sitting on the dashboard and the driver soon enlightened me by shaking powder onto the documents and gently blowing away the excess dust. We carefully edged closer and quickly realised the papers were actually GIRO cheques, the government payment system for unemployment benefit used in the day. They were blank and the men were completing the empty spaces with a fictitious name and random amounts under the £50 limit, which didn't require any form of I.D. for encashment at a Post Office. The tactic of using baby powder helped lessen the effect of the new black typewriter ribbon on the cheques. We watched them complete about ten cheques before deciding to pounce.

I said to Nev, "These two are kiting GIROS and they've obviously nicked them". (Kiting is a slang term for passing cheques as genuine) "Go to the passenger door and I'll give you the nod to go for it". I approached the driver's side and gave Nev the signal and we opened the doors at the same time. Both men were visibly shaken. I announced we were police officers, showing my warrant card. I said, "What you two up to?" Both replied in what I thought were Southern accents. Pc Edwards was engaged with his man and I asked the driver about who owned the car. He told me it was a friend's, but wouldn't name him. I immediately noticed the ignition contained an unusual shaped key and it didn't appear it was for that car.

I said, "You've nicked this car, haven't you." He didn't reply. At this moment I noticed his feet shuffling in the footwell as though trying to furtively move something. I told him to stay still and I reached down and discovered a Smith & Wesson .38 calibre handgun. My heart was beating faster with every beat; I'm wondering if he got hold of the weapon to use it on us or had he used it already. I grabbed it, and being firearms trained, quickly proved it as safe, removing six bullets from the chamber.

He said, "It's not mine, it was in the car."

I said, "Sure it was, why you trying to hide it then?"

Things were adding up to two travelling professional

criminals carrying a loaded gun. I called for backup as a matter of urgency, trying to keep things calm with small talk. It seemed to work, though neither man was incriminating himself very much. It was fortunate Pc Edwards had his handcuffs on him and with some reluctance, we cuffed them together until help arrived. Pc Edwards saw a white plastic carrier bag, partly secreted under the passenger seat and upon examination it was full of £20 and £10 notes. On first glance over a thousand pounds. We arrested them for firearms possession and conspiracy to defraud. They were conveyed to G Division DHQ at Frederick Street along with the car and other evidence. The passenger, realising he was in some trouble, suddenly blurted out he was an escapee from HMP Pentonville. His pal wasn't giving anything up. As much of the property recovered from their possession pointed to the Wandsworth area of London, I thought I would ring the Metropolitan Police who covered that area.

It was an instant hit. The detective I spoke with was simply elated to learn of the arrests, telling me our two men were the Kingpins in the massive burglary and theft of over a £1 million pounds worth of GIROS, cash and other goods A team of Met Detectives arrived the following day and scooped up the prisoners, together with the stolen car, stolen gun and ammo, and whisked them back to London. Subsequent enquiries led to the arrest of eight other men. Apart from the cash we had recovered, nothing else was found. The gang eventually stood trial at the Central Criminal Court in London, also known as

The Old Bailey. Pc Edwards and myself travelled by train from Doncaster to London Kings Cross, where our Met colleagues greeted us before taking us to a West End hotel, our base for the duration of the trial. We knew our services wouldn't be required for a few days, so our chaperone, a young Pc took us up to Heathrow Airport to see how the police station operated on the inside. Other doors were opened for us, with a fascinating tour around the BA Concorde check-in and lounges. Champagne, never tasted so good.

The trial began Monday and it was Thursday when we were listed to give evidence in Court Number 3. Although I'd given evidence at Assize Courts, Coroners Courts etc., this place was the high altar of them all. It is always daunting giving evidence anywhere, but here I was in the highest court in the land, standing in the oak panelled courtroom in the witness box, just feet away from the trial judge. It was the ultimate test of your professional capabilities as a witness. The defence barristers representing the gang made typical attacks, trying to discredit our evidence, but we stood firm and the jury found them all guilty of a range of crimes. The judge sentenced them all to identical terms of five years imprisonment.

All the Met. team of detectives, around twenty strong, together with Nev Edwards and myself adjourned to a private room set aside for police witnesses where handshakes and high-fives were exchanged to celebrate the end of a successful investigation. Nev and I had about an hour to return to our hotel and be ready for a 7pm pick up by armoured police coach which weaved its way through heavy traffic, taking us to the "Blind Beggar" pub on Whitechapel Road in the East End for pre-dinner drinks. It was a watering-hole for some Met. officers.

This Victorian public house gained infamy in the 1960's when George Cornell was shot to death in the public bar by notorious London gangster, Ronnie Kray. The landlord ramped up the mystique, saying Nev and I were standing in the spot where Cornell fell. After an aperitif or two we walked the few yards to Akhtar's Indian Restaurant on Brick Lane, where our table awaited us. Along with the Met. staff we enjoyed a convivial atmosphere in relaxed surroundings until violence erupted, as the three plate-glass windows of the eatery came crashing in, showering customers with broken glass. Four men had found dustbins and hurled them against the windows, shouting racist abuse as they did so. It proved to be an utterly foolhardy act, as within seconds about six chefs burst through the kitchen doors, armed with machetes, ready to confront the issue. The offenders were still shouting threats inviting people to fight them, saying, "Come on then if you want some." Although we'd all had a few drinks , we knew we had to act quickly to avert a potential bloodbath, as the weapons being wielded by the staff could inflict fearsome injury. Some of our group managed to calm the cooks and the rest of us snuffed out the threat by detaining the offenders until the police came and carted them away to the local nick. A sort of Indian Takeaway so to speak. It was a stroke of real good fortune for this gang of idiots, for if the private police party hadn't been held there, and no-one had intervened, they could have regretted their senseless actions for the rest of their lives, if indeed they had lived to do so. I knew these cooks meant business!

So, an eventful week in the capital was at an end as we packed our bags and caught our train at King's Cross Station. The following week, Nev and I and our divisional officer, Chief Superintendent Devine, who provided us with a bitter-sweet moment handing us written commendations on behalf of the Commissioner of Police for the Metropolitan Police, followed by disciplinary papers alleging assault by all four of the dustbin throwers who were later convicted of criminal damage and affray. They'd had the temerity to complain, perhaps failing to recognise the group of policemen had perhaps saved their lives. They later saw sense and withdrew their complaints.

Pc Frank Phillips returned from Asia and took possession of his car. He was close to tears.

Chapter 15
Crime Wave

Colin Ronald Albert Broadfoot was born in 1950 in Manchester. He had a formidable criminal history, with convictions for major burglaries, GBH, false pretences, car theft and assault on police. He had served several lengthy prison sentences and was a plausible, cunning villain, who lived on his wits and avoided gainful employment at all costs. At a recent court appearance in Sheffield his lawyer had hoodwinked the magistrate into putting Broadfoot on probation for handling stolen goods. The court was told he intended to leave the city and start a new crime free life in Rotherham. The Chairman of the Bench wished him good luck in his bid to go straight. As if.

The Crime Intelligence Officer at Snig Hill, Sheffield, notified his Rotherham counterpart that a crime wave was coming the 10 miles down the road. I was in CID in G Division, of Sheffield and Rotherham Constabulary when I attended a joint CID/Uniform crime talk which covered current crime trends, wanted criminals and other related police matters. Mr Broadfoot featured in a talk, complete with his photograph and antecedent history. It was only a few weeks before Broadfoot's promise to go straight evaporated and he returned to his old criminal ways.

His MO (modus operandi) to commit offences changed little. He was a creature of habit. He was very devious and sought out young uniform constables to impress them with his tall stories of being a big player in the criminal underworld. He'd invite them to his Wellgate house and regale them with his lies and deceit and try to discover about local police practices, manpower deployment and other confidential information, all useful to him. To inflate his big time ego he had a personalised registration plate on his Mercedes car – CRB 1. He had acquired a stolen VEL (Vehicle Excise Licence) which he expertly immersed in brake fluid, which magically caused the original handwritten details to disappear, before writing his own details on the disc. In the days before instant computer checks, he gambled that any police checks wouldn't extend to DVLA. Mr Broadfoot was so brazen, he would commit burglary at various times of day, always using his car to plunder shops. He became careless and was arrested on numerous occasions in and around Rotherham, by uniformed and CID officers.

The process then was that all criminal related matters were the responsibility of the duty detectives to handle and prepare court papers. Broadfoot was being dealt with by at least six detectives including me. The DCI observed that manpower was being drained by this one-man crime wave, as he would always elect trial by jury, which was a long and time consuming event. The DCI (Detective Chief

Inspector) decided to nominate one detective to deal with Broadfoot. No matter what time of day, this officer would have that sole responsibility. We were all dreading getting the short straw and the CID office fell silent until the senior officer named DC Derek Tomlinson as the chosen one. There were many audible sighs of relief from the rest of the office staff.

Broadfoot quickly learned that Tomlinson would be in the opposite corner so to speak. They had met and there was no love lost; with the burglar openly threatening to "do him one day" and with his previous convictions for assaults, particularly on police officers, we all took his statement as no idle threat. A couple of encounters quickly followed, as Broadfoot hadn't the sense to draw a line under criminal activities. He was a marked man now. The CID officers occasionally had a departmental evening out and often chose a quiet venue where we could relax relatively undisturbed. The Oasis club at Kimberworth was an ideal location. Most of the team had been on a daytime shift and met up at the club. The seating plan consisted of "lobster pot" design wicker furniture, tables and chairs. I was standing near the bar area talking to DC Mel Taylor, who pointed out Derek Tomlinson and his wife seated at a table at the back of the room. They were holding hands and seemed besotted with each other. Derek went to the men's room and suddenly Broadfoot strode quickly to their table. Someone had tipped Broadfoot about our evening out. He started verbally abusing Mrs Tomlinson, saying about Derek, "He's a bent bastard. I'm gunna have him."At that point we were joined by the club's commissionaire, Dougie Taylor, bedecked in his full uniform and red sash, who also witnessed Broadfoot's rant. The ensuing moments happened very quickly, as Derek returned to the table. His face etched with anger, he said, "What the fuck you doing talking to my wife?"

Broadfoot was on a mission and he quickly attacked, throwing a wild right cross, which brushed Derek's eyebrow. Derek weighed in with a powerful right to his jaw, snapping Broadfoot's head back. We somehow thought Broadfoot's head had been literally knocked off his shoulders, but as we tracked its movement, we quickly realised it was his toupee, which had become airborne at pace. Derek repelled his attacker's futile efforts to launch more blows and responded with a barrage of his own, to end all resistance. We intervened to calm the situation and returned Broadfoot's toupee to his head. He knew he had been the aggressor and had come off second best.

The following day I was deputed to take a witness statement from Dr Paul at A&E Doncaster Gate Hospital, Rotherham. It listed Broadfoot's extensive injuries, running to five pages. DC Tomlinson's injury was minor by comparison. Upon his discharge from hospital, Broadfoot was remanded in custody and appeared before the Crown Court, drawing a three years term of imprisonment for his criminal spree, including assault on DC Tomlinson and theft of the VEL he had used on his car illegally. He received a wigging from the judge as he was taken to the cells.

Upon his release, Broadfoot decided to leave Rotherham for good. Perhaps finally realising that crime doesn't pay.

Chapter 16
Victim Of A Serial Killer

Once a serial killer has a victim in his sights, it's really a matter of his choosing when a life will end. Dennis Nilsen was born in 1945 in Scotland. He killed, defiled and dismembered fifteen young men and became known as The Muswell Hill Murderer. He joined the army at 16 and became a cook, serving as a butcher in the catering corps, learning skills that served him so well during his five year killing spree. Upon leaving the services in 1972, he joined the police, where he discovered a fascination with morgue visits and autopsied bodies! He later resigned and became an interviewer. Nilsen was homosexual, as were many of his victims. He preyed on the homeless and unemployed. He'd lure them back to his flat, have sex with them, often plying them with alcohol before killing them, usually by strangulation. He would donate their clothing and dismember their bodies on the stone floor. Nilsen boiled the heads of victims to remove the flesh from their skulls. At one time Nilsen had six bodies in various rooms in his flat. They were in different states of decomposition, and to eliminate the smell of rotting flesh, and the army of flies, he used aerosol sprays.

In 1972 I was a detective officer in Rotherham CID, when the father of Malcolm Barlow reported to me the theft of his unemployment GIRO cheque, amounting to a couple of pounds. He alleged his son, Malcolm had admitted to him that he had cashed it and spent the money on alcohol. The Barlow family consisted of Mr & Mrs Barlow and at least six sons who were spaced in ages about a year apart. They were all remarkably similar in features and build. They reminded me of the Russian type Matryoshka stacking doll; a large doll containing several others, descending in size. The family lived in a council rented semi-detached house on a large estate close to the Rotherham town centre and were entirely dependent on state benefits according to Malcolm. I was unable to process him at that stage, so released him on bail to return to the police station. However he jumped bail and left town. Accordingly I officially circulated him as a wanted person in a national publication called The Police Gazette, in the days before computers. Some weeks went by without sight or sound of the fugitive, until I received a telephone call from sergeant Jack Joll of the Sussex Constabulary, saying Barlow had surrendered himself at Bognor Regis police station. The prisoner had enough intelligence to realise although he had no funds, this was a sure way of getting a free one way ticket home. I journeyed to the coastal town with a colleague to collect Barlow. We stayed overnight and my police colleagues accorded us their hospitality by taking us out for a drink, as was custom and practice in those days for visiting officers from other forces.

The following day we took possession of Barlow and his property and commenced our journey home. Barlow seemed happy to see us and confided he'd been sleeping rough and wanted to get home. The British Rail carriage had separate compartments and our colleagues from the British Transport Police provided us with our own private one, with a "Police Do Not Disturb" sign on the door. Barlow slept almost all the way back to Sheffield, where we were met and driven to Rotherham. The prisoner was interviewed, charged, and put to bed in his cell ahead of his court appearance before the local Magistrates Court the following day. He pleaded guilty to theft and received a small fine. I'm sure the cost of our wages, return travel, accommodation, and subsistence far outweighed his penalty, but that's how things operated over forty years ago.

The next I heard of Barlow was in September 1981, when I learned he'd gone to London to seek a better life for himself. He found himself in an unfamiliar area of the capital, where he took ill; suffering an epileptic episode. Barlow was semi-conscious and was slumped against a wall, when a Good Samaritan came to his aid, but his rescuer turned out to be the devil incarnate, Dennis Nilsen. Nilsen called for an ambulance and Barlow was detained overnight in hospital. It's not clear how or why Barlow returned to see Nilsen, but he did. Barlow was invited into Nilsen's flat at 195 Melrose Grove, where he ate his last meal before he was plied with rum and coke by the mass killer and necrophiliac. The stricken Yorkshireman was cynically being readied for the slaughter and would soon become another routine, easy killing by the deranged Scot. Every room in the flat contained a decaying dead body, and Nilsen faced a disposal dilemma with his latest victim. He cleared out the area beneath the sink and roughly pushed Barlow into the small space to leave him resembling an embryo in the womb. Other body parts after dismemberment were burned on bonfires or flushed down the toilet, causing the drains to become blocked.

Nilsen was tried at The Old Bailey. He pleaded not guilty to a catalogue of horrific crimes, but was duly convicted and sentenced to life imprisonment, later replaced by a whole life tariff by the Home Secretary.

Ironically, a former school classmate of mine has a son who is a jailer at HMP Full Sutton York, where Nilsen was incarcerated and he supervised him as he spent his days reading and writing and composing music on his keyboard. The killer also exchanged letters with numerous people who sought his correspondence.

The hapless Malcolm Barlow has the unenviable distinction of being a victim of the second highest known serial killer in British criminal history, behind Doctor Harold Shipman; with a suspected count of 260.

Nilsen died on 13th May 2018.

Chapter 17
The Matador

Yet another amalgamation took place in 1974 when Sheffield and Rotherham Constabulary combined with other local forces to become South Yorkshire Police, including part of the old West Riding Police.

I was promoted to Sergeant in 1977 and I was transferred to Rawmarsh sub division. Living in the sub division it was only two miles to work. I knew the area well and many people who lived there. One summer's night I was working 10pm – 6am. The Green Lane police station had the office in the control room and Pc Graham and Pc Young out on foot patrol. Around 11.30pm we were all at the station when a member of the public called in and reported a major disturbance at The Matador Club on Chapel Street, just over the road beyond a row of houses. I knew the club was a former church hall, primarily used for tea dances and bingo sessions. We three made our way on foot to the hall arriving in about 3 minutes to see numerous men milling about outside. We entered the premises one by one to encounter maybe fifty or so men in small groups.

Walking through the large hall, I soon realised there was lots of broken glass on the floor over a wide area. Tables were upturned along with several wooden chairs. I saw a man walk to a table containing several part consumed beer glasses. He proceeded to pick them up and throw them at the quadrant shaped public bar in the corner of the room. It was like a coconut shy at a fairground. Each one he threw broke an array of optics, bottles and glasses. I grabbed his arm as he was preparing to throw another, telling him I was arresting him for causing criminal damage. He began to struggle and was shouting and swearing and was obviously drunk. I was fearful if I fell on the floor during the melee, I'd surely sustain serious lacerations from the broken glass. Mayhem broke out and several men attacked my two colleagues, who both finished up on the ground clutching their faces from blows they'd received. I had control of my man, when I suddenly felt a hand go down the back of my shirt collar and a voice say, "Get off him or I'll kill thee." I'm 6ft and this man towered above me. I guessed he was 20 stone. I tried to grapple with him, but three of his mates joined in and put me on the deck, allowing my prisoner to escape. Within a few moments the hall had cleared. We managed to get a 10–9 radio call in for assistance, but it was about 15 minutes before help arrived from Rotherham. The streets had cleared and the hall was empty. We licked our wounds and returned to the station. Luckily our injuries were superficial, but could have been so much worse.

Local enquires revealed that the cause of the disorder was to do with the organisers wanting the all male gathering to pay extra to their entrance fee to have the female striptease artistes do an encore with selected members of the already drunken mob, taking an active role on the stage with the strippers. Their refusal to pay sparked the fighting and bottle throwing.

I thought perhaps a trawl on the streets might yield some stragglers making their way home and bingo it did. I enlisted the aid of a CID officer in a plain car to drive slowly up Haugh Road, where we saw a woman and two men walking slowly up the street, with the man on the outside conscious enough to catch a glimpse of our vehicle. He kept glancing back and it suddenly dawned on me that he was none other than my escaped glass thrower. We exited the car and approached them and before we could speak, my man blurted out, "We've not been to The Matador, if that's what you think." Classic line for sure.

I cautioned him and rearrested him for his wrecking spree and transported him to the police station. After the big cell door clanged shut, within seconds he was ringing the cell call bell wanting to cooperate. He was well aware who organised the event, supplying me with names, especially the name of the man who had assaulted me. So things were starting to take shape and by 3 am, the 6 foot 9 inch police attacker was answering his door in his boxer shorts, totally denying everything about The Matador incident. His wife appeared in her rollers, demanding to know the score. I promptly told her that her beloved had been involved in the arrangement of a striptease show. She went berserk and started beating on his chest, calling him from a pig to a dog. He looked at me as if to say, please lock me up and get me away from her. We did just that.

We were on a roll by now and soon had more names confirmed and two more were detained before daylight broke. The sins of the flesh and the demon drink had come back to haunt them all. By mid afternoon all four men were facing charges of assaulting three policemen, affray and criminal damage. They all pleaded guilty and received large fines and were also ordered to pay each of us compensation of £2.50p; a total of £10. Their convictions meant much more than money to us.

Chapter 18
Mass Murderer

Bank Holiday Monday 29th August 1988 was a lovely sunny day in South Yorkshire. I was the duty inspector at Rawmarsh Police Station, sitting at my desk, checking through paperwork when I went through to the control room to collect a report and the main switchboard illuminated with an incoming call. I clicked the switch to activate it, announced myself and heard a female reply in a calm voice, "Can you come down to Wath, I've just found my son murdered." I was taken aback momentarily as it's rare to hear such a matter of fact statement. I asked her if she was the birth mother, she confirmed she was and told me she'd wait at the semi-detached bungalow at Denman Road until we arrived. I kept an open mind until I could confirm her claim.

Together with the duty CID officer, Det Sgt Metcalfe, we drove the short distance to Wath, to see Mrs Law standing outside the residence. She showed no visible signs of emotion and appeared just normal. We could see the front of the address had no obvious signs of forced entry, but as I descended the concrete path towards the door, I saw a man's wrist watch half way up the tiled roof of the single storey property. Mrs Law hadn't seen her son, Marcus for a

112

couple of days and she had gone to visit him. She directed us into the main living room, which was the scene of utter carnage, the like I had never witnessed before in 25 years police service. I had often experienced the unmistakeable smell of "death" and it pervaded the small room as we conducted a cursory examination of the body and general crime scene.

Marcus Law was a partial invalid, due to a motorcycle accident which left him with leg injuries. He used a wheelchair and could get about using crutches. He was laid on his back, his shirt had been pushed up to his upper chest and his trousers were pulled down to knee level, exposing that area of his body, which had been the target area for the murderer's furious onslaught. A straight clean vertical cut had been made from the chest area to the lower abdomen and he had been disembowelled. Scores of stab wounds were visible on the body. One crutch had been driven into a gaping wound. Law's eyes had also been gouged out. The deceased had five cigarettes inserted into his face: one in each eye socket, one in each nostril, and one between his lips. Mrs Law remained with us throughout. She still remained calm and collected despite discovering her birth son had been butchered in such horrific circumstances. I couldn't help wondering what sort of person could commit such an inhuman act against another and inflict over seventy stab wounds in this killing frenzy. Large blue bottle flies were being attracted to the body, as it started decomposing.

This was now a major crime scene and evidence

needed to be secured and preserved, so I had constables positioned at the front and rear of the property. It was a relief to get outside into the fresh air, to clear my airways of the smell of death. We initiated the major incident chain of command to Detective Chief Superintendent level and soon this quiet avenue would see the full effect of the Forces Murder Team.

Logistically they would have the town's police station within a few yards of the scene which was a decided advantage in the initial stages of the investigation.

Word on the street from numerous people suggested Anthony Arkwright could be the killer and he was immediately declared South Yorkshire's "MOST WANTED" in connection with this crime. Arkwright was quickly arrested and initially detained at Rawmarsh Police Station under 24 hour guard. His cell had been fitted with covert CCTV and audio and his every move recorded.

Raymond Ford, a near neighbour in Wath, was later discovered savagely murdered, also disembowelled and stabbed over 250 times, with his entrails draped around the room.

During his cell time, Arkwright asked for a deck of playing cards, which he shuffled and placed them on a table separately, saying, "The four of hearts. I see that card four of hearts." It transpired he meant his four victims and soon after his grandfather and his housekeeper were found murdered in the neighbouring town of Mexborough. Although he was never convicted of the woman's death, the case was ordered to lie on the file.

Arkwright was jailed for a recommended 25 years and the Home Secretary reviewed his case and imposed a whole life tariff, never to be released. In 2014 Arkwright appealed and three high court judges rejected the appeal, ruling the whole life tariff was completely lawful.

Why did Arkwright kill? Notwithstanding his deprived childhood, he craved infamy and would have loved nothing more than to have been one of Britain's most reviled killers, but for all of his horrific crimes, the name of Anthony Arkwright never made it into the public consciousness like the Yorkshire Ripper, Peter Sutcliffe, who he so desperately wanted to emulate. The killer has never expressed any emotion or remorse for his actions. Arkwright's name is hardly remembered, even largely unknown, but the families of his victims will never forget his horrific actions.

14 years after his son's murder, Marcus Law's father, Tony, committed suicide by gassing himself in his car, he had never got over his son's death. The wrist watch found on the roof of Denman Road, belonged to Marcus and had been taken by Arkwright, who like all his victims, he regarded as having no value, he tossed the timepiece onto the roof.

An officer concerned with the murder enquiry commissioned a company to make a navy blue necktie available to all personnel connected with the investigation. It carried a picture of a playing card, 'The Four of Hearts'.

This action is called "Gallows Humour". It treats serious, frightening or painful matters in a light or satirical way. Unless you've been a first responder in the emergency services like the police, or my old pals Derek Mastin and Derek Kirk, of the Borough Ambulance and Fire Service respectively and dealt with the daily horrors of life, you may never comprehend. It's not to dismiss or diminish the seriousness of the matter, or the pain or loss the victim and their families have suffered; it's a form of coping strategy to try and deal with the psychological traumas. Police officers are human beings, they have to go home after a tour of duty and carry what they have seen with them. Their loved ones and close friends act as their counsellors. There's no "Return to factory settings" or "Delete" button on your brain like a computer has. You carry the memories for life. The police are a benign brotherhood of dedicated officers operating in an ever more dangerous world.

Chapter 19
The Hillsborough Disaster

In football terms the South Yorkshire is a hotbed of football rivalries, having five professional clubs operating in different leagues. They are -

Sheffield United
Sheffield Wednesday
Rotherham United
Barnsley
Doncaster Rovers

My first experience as a policeman at a professional game was at Millmoor ground, home of Rotherham United in January 1966, when they replayed an FA cup-tie, losing 2–1 to a star-studded Manchester United team, fielding, Law, Charlton, Best, Stiles and co. In those days, Rotherham regularly had a 12000 crowd supporting them, which was policed by a Sergeant and three Constables. It was common for visiting fans to stand shoulder to shoulder with the home supporters and friendships were forged, Public disorder was a rarity, arrests unheard of, and if anyone was unruly a word in their ear always did the trick.

The scourge of UK soccer hooliganism later

plagued the national game, and violence and disorder proliferated on many grounds, resulting in escalation of police manpower to combat this rising phenomenon. From requiring only a few officers to police large crowds, things altered dramatically with many forces creating dedicated departments to deal with soccer related matters, as violence escalated at soccer matches. In addition to increased manpower, they were supplemented with mounted police, dog handlers, helicopters and use of CCTV. Mass public disorder, often well orchestrated, has a huge effect upon police resources. I'm sure many more arrests could be made at these events, but it would be counter productive and weaken the thin blue line even further.

In the late eighties, I was an Inspector at Rawmarsh. The FA Cup was at the semi-final stage and brought together Liverpool and Nottingham Forest. The neutral venue for the tie was Hillsborough; the home of Sheffield Wednesday. It had staged many similar games before, and large crowds were not uncommon at this venue. A match order would be prepared. Every force order followed the same blueprint, using the same mnemonic: IIMAC – Information – Intention – Method – Administration – Control. So it was entirely feasible that the previous order was used and the names and dates changed to update it. Superintendent Bernard Murray, who was my sub divisional officer, was chosen Match Commander, David Duckenfield's deputy at the game.

On Wednesday 12th April, a senior officers'

briefing was held in the gymnasium at the ground. I attended, where I received a copy of the match orders. I had policed numerous games at Hillsborough in the past, which was an advantage in many ways. The police match Commander for Hillsborough, Chief Superintendent Brian Mole, had been Divisional Officer of E Division, which covered the stadium. He had overseen several semi-final ties, as well as league and cup fixtures at the stadium during his time there, but weeks before the 15th April 1989 game, he had been transferred to Barnsley for a "career development move". This was as a result of fallout following a police prank, involving his officers on a night duty shift, during which a probationary constable was blindfolded, handcuffed and, it was said, threatened with a gun. The prank was later re-enacted in a TV programme which tried to highlight the link between Mole's transfer and Duckenfield's introduction to match Commander status, as a major factor in the disaster. The move was only about three weeks before the day of the disaster.

Mole's rank carried vicarious liability for the personnel under his command, who let him down in spectacular fashion, with a cluster of officers involved in the brainless conspiracy of madness which led to their Commander's transfer, four of them being required to resign and seven others being disciplined.

This scenario increased speculation that if Mole had remained in post, the disaster may not have happened. It also brought into sharp focus the decision of the force hierarchy to promote Duckenfield into a senior command role that he patently wasn't ready for.

On the fateful day, the hundreds of officers involved in the match detail paraded at various Divisions force-wide, including some officers who worked in office situations and had not been involved in operation duties for one reason or another for many years. In effect they were making up the required numbers. Local bus companies were enlisted to transport officers to the stadium in Sheffield by 11am.

We mustered into our prearranged serials, comprising an Inspector, Sergeants and Constables and formed up in the host club's gymnasium, located within the ground at Penistone Road. The match commander, Chief Supt. Duckenfield, reiterated the general content of the match order. The obvious intention was for the game to go off without any major incidents and it was hoped the police and supporters would maintain a convivial rapport, on a lovely spring day, but within hours, the disaster unfolded, resulting in mass deaths of unbelievable proportions. The events especially around kick off time have been well documented over the years.

Hillsborough will forever be synonymous with the worst stadium disaster in English sporting history, resulting in the 96 Liverpool supporters' horrific deaths through crush injuries, and hundreds more injured and traumatised. This was after a series of alleged fatal errors by those in charge of ensuring the safety of those attending.

After completion of the first phase of the match order, I left the ground with my serial and had just reached Penistone Road, when we were directed to go inside. It was the most surreal unexpected sight. Hundreds of people were milling about on the pitch in utter chaos. Like millions of others over the years, I've seen television pictures repeating the events of that day.

I don't recall receiving any direction from the Police Commander as I joined scores of other officers at the security fence at the Leppings Lane end. Everyone there were doing their utmost to help people trapped in the pens. Some were lifted over the high fence onto the playing surface. Advertising boards were being used to carry people on. It was like a scene from a war zone, you'd expect to see on the TV news.

I will refrain from commenting upon my personal views concerning the Liverpool so-called supporters' involvement in these tragic events, out of respect to dead and their families, who have undoubtedly suffered beyond measure in the aftermath of a disaster which came to haunt English football for decades to come.

I remember, amidst the mayhem, talking to ground control within the stadium, as it appeared the fans at either end didn't appear to know exactly what was happening. I approached Kenny Dalglish and Brian Clough, the respective managers of Liverpool and Nottingham Forest, who agreed to make Tannoy appeals for calm, which seemed to be heeded for a short time at least. Following the match stoppage at

3.06.30secs, time seemed to freeze; it was quite surreal being there.

It was probably after 5pm when I walked across the pitch, which was scattered with broken billboards, scarves, bobble hats and police helmets. I picked my way over to the gymnasium.

The sights and sounds witnessed in there will haunt me forever; the symmetrical arrangement of the dozens of white body bags, all with facial observation panels. I saw some policemen kneeling by the bags, maybe writing information on pieces of paper. The effects of the post mortem degradation of the bodies within the gymnasium was beginning to take place and despite them being contained in zipped bags, the unmistakable smell of death pervaded the air. The whole scenario was like being awake in an horrendous dream. No police training had prepared me for such a disaster. We were all in the same situation. People, including police, were walking about zombie-like, trying to comprehend the magnitude of being involved.

I looked around and wondered how a football match, on a lovely spring day in England could end in utter carnage. It occurred to me that these people would never go home. How would their loved ones react; endless thoughts resonated in my mind.

Subsequent to the disaster, the Taylor report was produced which made safety measures mandatory at stadia throughout the land and is a lasting legacy to the memory of those innocents who perished at Hillsborough.

There exists today, despite the events of

John Newey

Hillsborough, a perverse mentality, whereby some people masquerading as football supporters, who refuse to recognise and acknowledge their personal, moral and legal duty to conform to the laws of the land cannot go out individually or en masse and behave irresponsibly. All too often they resort to trying to shift their own shameless shortcomings onto someone else and it's the police who are usually held to account. Life is short. Memories are very much shorter, or so it seems.

Chapter 20
American Pit Bull Terrier

In the autumn of 1991, I was at home watching BBC TV, Look North news, when they covered a story involving a middle aged man enjoying a picnic in a Lincoln park.

He saw an unaccompanied American Pit Bull Terrier dog and offered it some of his food. It proved to be a life changing decision he would regret. He was sitting on the grass when the dog lunged at him, locking onto his nose and biting it off. The man has now to wear a prosthetic nose for the rest of his life. The 'Dangerous Dogs Act 1991' had been recently enacted by Parliament, who had recognised the serious dangers presented to the public by such animals. Certain elements of the community felt that having ownership of such a fearsome animal gave them added kudos.

On Thursday 1st October 1991, I was Duty Inspector at Rawmarsh Police Station, when a member of the public reported three young children had been attacked by a rogue American Pit Bull Terrier in the Thrybergh area of Rotherham. The children had all been bitten by the dog, one seriously. They had sought refuge in a telephone box to escape from the dog. Two constables were despatched to the scene and I followed soon afterwards, taking an old pair of motorcycle gauntlets and a snare pole with me. No similar incidents had occurred in the force area hitherto, therefore no provision had been made to deal with anything of a similar nature. I reached the scene to learn the children had been conveyed to hospital. The dog was sitting on an open plan garden, as the street began to fill with people. Prior to leaving the station, I had instructed the office man to request the attendance of a firearms officer via Force HQ, where firearms were kept back in the day. The office man replied, "I thought you were joking, so I haven't done it!" I was furious he hadn't complied. I told him again to do it and update me.

Thrybergh was predominantly a mining community with many people employed at the nearby Silverwood colliery, later to close in 1994. The 1984 miners' strike was still fresh in the minds of many and the police weren't popular by any means. Shirtless tattooed men were shouting derogatory remarks and the atmosphere was becoming hostile. I appealed for anyone with a net so I could contain the dog, but not unexpectedly my appeal fell on deaf ears. A stroke of good fortune came to my aid, when a man came by with his Staffordshire Bull Terrier bitch. He told me his animal was "on heat" and he knew enough about dogs to advise me the Pit Bull would be attracted to his pet; but for how long was anyone's guess. It bought me some valuable time to access further options.

The street sideshow was attracting more people and I heard a man shout, "Do something you useless bastards". I had very few options available, so decided to employ the snare noose pole. I donned the gauntlets, checked the blue nylon cord, which was misshapen due to lack of use and it occurred to me that I would only get one shot at successfully capturing the dog. I rehearsed my technique in my mind over and over, before taking aim. I had opened the noose to a wide circle. I naturally felt anxious, but had to remain composed. The dog thankfully remained sitting on the grass perfectly still, when I lassoed its neck with my first shot. My heart was pounding, my knees knocking, as I rammed the pole into its throat and tightened the nylon cord around its neck. I was just inches from the snarling dog's fearsome jaws, it was now fighting for its life and was hell bent on escaping, but I had to keep hold. I was now on my knees, with my arms straight and my elbows locked out. I could see my arms shaking, but I dare not relax as I could suffer the same fate as the man from Lincoln, or even worse. The dog was foaming at the mouth as I exerted all my strength to prevail in this epic encounter.

It was paramount I had to protect the public and eventually the dog expired through strangulation. It was regrettable but necessary. I was all in, my body shaking like a leaf. The body of the Pit Bull was placed into a bin liner and into the boot of the police car. The crowd shuffled off in different directions, no congratulations offered, none expected.

My police radio crackled into life, "Message for

Inspector Newey. Firearms Officer authorised and attending. ETA 2 hours". I was told the authorised firearms man lived in Derbyshire and would have to call at West Bar Police Station in Sheffield to collect a weapon en route to me. With the passage of time, provisions have been made to deal with similar incidents in a more professional manner. Armed response vehicles are available 24/7

I replied to my radio call, "Cancel all units, matter resolved. Resuming patrol". The dog was weighed and was over 5 stones. It had no identification and an owner was never found.

The following day I was at the police station when ITV, BBC, and various national newspapers descended for interviews and photographs.

Initially I had no perception of the extent of my injuries, but CAT Scans and X Rays revealed I had extensive damage to my neck, shoulders and three fractures to my third, fourth and fifth lumbar spine. As opposed to the straw that broke the camel's back, this was the Pit Bull that broke the policeman's back.

The children were released after treatment, their injuries minor, and hopefully their mental scars will have healed by now.

Chapter 21
The Beginning Of The End

The fat lady could be heard warming up her vocal cords – I knew it was time to quit.

A few days after the dangerous dog incident which seriously injured my back - although I didn't know the extent of the injury at that time - my Sub Divisional Commander, Superintendent Bernard Murray arranged to conduct my annual staff appraisal at Rawmarsh Police Station. He had been second in command at the Hillsborough Disaster and was heavily preoccupied in the aftermath, and I truly sympathised with his position. I'm sure trying to run a sub division, whilst wrestling with the fallout of such a catastrophic event proved a difficult task for him. I was surprised when he told me he thought an Operational Inspector should be more admin minded and not being involved in arresting people! Then he referred to another complaint against me by a career criminal who complained about every officer he encountered – I guessed he was predisposed towards the opposition? He, his deputy and at least two of my peers were ex training department personnel, fully supportive of the political correctness route. I was more on the side of arresting criminals.

I thought the appraisal was going nowhere, then he dropped his bombshell, that he was proposing to transfer me to Maltby in a swap for another inspector, as his shift was a shambles and it needed a strong character to straighten it out. Which was me! I said laughingly that it was Rawmarsh that was the shambles in need of straightening out, with one Inspector wanting to return to join his pals in Sheffield, and another reportedly doing an Open University course in duty time. His dissertation was completed by the station typist on paid overtime, authorised by the Superintendent!

I remember the mantra impressed on new recruits at training school being honesty, loyalty, truthfulness and courage. The police discipline code created offences, including falsehood and prevarication – what a contradiction in terms. I was never treacherous in all my service. Yes, I expected high standards in commitment, appearance and performance, as most managers would. Some wicked, devious policemen thrived upon despicable acts of treachery against their colleagues, all too often escaping any disciplinary action.

I believe my police career prospects came to a shuddering halt in the summer of 1983 and it involved a game of golf at Rotherham Golf Club. Outside the club house I saw two men; one was William Arthur, a police traffic superintendent, based at Doncaster. I knew him by sight, but had never met him before. The other man was the then Mayor of Rotherham, Joe Allott JP. I'd seen him around town but hadn't met him.

We agreed to play a round together. In all my service I had never been involved in idle gossip on or off duty, but I would soon learn that my two golfing colleagues were well versed in the dark art of back stabbing others. They appeared to know who I was and within a few yards from the first tee, the Mayor was firing questions at me about my knowledge of a certain Superintendent called Ron Norden, who I knew well over many years. I had the greatest respect for him as a practical policeman, who had been instrumental in my promotion to the rank of Inspector and had intimated I would rejoin him when an opportunity arose. I had worked with Ron when I was the Area Sergeant at Rotherham and had accompanied him on a number of enquiries, as far away as Scotland. The Mayor was obviously aware that Norden was associating with a policewoman who he later married, and he was really anxious to know all about him. I avoided every question, saying I knew nothing about his private life, when William Arthur chimed in, saying he disliked Norden intensely, reeling off a series of scurrilous allegations about a brother officer of equal rank. I was appalled and told him of my respect for the man. I had gone out for a relaxing game of golf on a summers day and here I was listening to two twisted gossip mongers. Was I glad to reach the 18th green and go home.

I hadn't given much thought to this encounter until a few days later, when I had a chat with the golf professional at the club, when he told me Ron Norden had asked him who I played golf with. I thought it was an unusual enquiry to make, so I called into Main Street Police Station to see Ron Norden. We had a full and frank discussion about my meeting with Arthur and Allott. Norden then told me he was disappointed that I had sought to speak disparagingly about him. I was truly gob-smacked when he recounted what Arthur had told him. The gutless coward had attributed his own slanderous remarks to me. I thought Why? What was his motive to discredit me - someone he didn't know? It was as perverse as it was pernicious. I thought Ron would recognise my reaction as honest and sincere, but despite assuring me he believed my protestations, I knew he didn't. I went to get a car and both drive over and confront the evil Arthur, but Ron told me to forget it.

I thought long and hard about taking my case to the top level, The Chief Constable, but knowing the inner circle's workings, I thought I may win the battle but not the war. How could such wickedness be allowed to happen and go unpunished? The battle on the streets was difficult in the extreme, with dangers looming around every corner, but more serious danger existed in the corridors of police stations.

The South Yorkshire Police in recent years has stumbled from one self-inflicted crisis to another, weakening its ability to fight genuine crime. It's a force that for too long has been gripped by a dangerous cocktail of poor leadership, politically correct dogma, warped priorities and tactical incompetence. Only an organisation obsessed with the creed of diversity and lacking in moral integrity, would have allowed the likes of Arthur and others to gain senior positions. It was widely reported Mr Arthur was the commander of the traffic department based at the Sprotborough Police Post, adjacent to the A1(M) near Doncaster when some of his officers decided, in duty time, to launch the Force Film Festival event. They held regular pornographic shows at the post, which were said to be well attended by local officers and some from neighbouring forces. I wondered if they had an usher etc., carrying a tray with Kia-Ora juice and Butterkist at the interval.

In yet another case which shamed South Yorkshire Police, a constable christened by colleagues as "Team Deviant" filmed couples "dogging", which is a slang term for couples engaging in sexual activities in a public place, which brings a whole new meaning to "The Chopper Squad"!

Too many senior officers have forgotten their central role is to protect the law-abiding British public. Instead of taking tough decisions, they indulge in politicised manoeuvres designed to protect their own backs and further their own careers.

The high command in some forces inhabits a culture where cowardice is dressed up as pragmatism, where a talent for spouting buzz words and sound-bites beats the determination to take on the bad guys. The British citizens are once again the losers, as are the officers on the beat, often doing a heroic, selfless job, being undermined by their selfish, conceited, career driven superiors. A well known saying in police circles about some senior management, involving the men and women at the sharp end, is that they are lions led by donkeys. The public expect and demand that these leaders of men, being paid high wages, are accountable for controversial decisions and should not be paralysed by political correctness. The Rotherham child sex abuse crimes involving 1400 girls is a case in point. Failures of police and others proved to be catastrophic.

When my serious back injury didn't respond to treatment in 1992, I retired from the police on medical grounds,being deemed unable/unfit to perform operational duties, but the then Chief Constable, Richard Wells was very supportive, asking me to consider an office job at HQ. I politely declined.

All organisations depend on a solid infrastructure where every member is as equally important as the next. That includes all police support staff, cleaners, mechanics etc., right up the ladder to the Chief Constable. Three officers I served with were knighted:

Sir Norman Bettison, was a cadet in my Rotherham CID days, later becoming Chief Constable of Merseyside, West Yorkshire.

Sir Bernard Hogan-Howe, I served at Mexborough with: Chief Constable of Merseyside and the Commissioner of the Metropolitan Police. He's now a Lord.

Sir Keith Povey, my Chief Inspector at Hackenthorpe, Sheffield, former Chief Constable of Leicestershire and Northamptonshire, then became Her Majesty's Inspector of Constabulary.

They were at the top of the police pyramid and Pc 251 Phillips at its foundation but, to me, he will always be as equally important as them.

My service spanned four decades and I saw many changes during that time. I was very sad to leave, having enjoyed meeting so many people. I was proud of my public service. So many things have changed since I joined over a half a century ago, notably the uniform with cops looking so paramilitary now. Often seen hatless, or wearing baseball caps instead. and their waist belts carry tazers and pepper spray, amongst other equipment. I hope they will never be routinely armed, but I fear in time they might be.

It was an honour to serve our Sovereign Lady the Queen, and the community of South Yorkshire, especially Rotherham Borough.

John Newey

29972589R00082

Printed in Poland
by Amazon Fulfillment
Poland Sp. z o.o., Wrocław